Just Money

D1639039

Just Money

Mission-Driven Banks and the Future of Finance

Katrin Kaufer and Lillian Steponaitis

The MIT Press

Cambridge, Massachusetts | London, England

This book was set in Stone Serif and Stone Sans by Westchester Publishing Services. Printed and bound in the United States of America.

Library of Congress Cataloging-in-Publication Data

Names: Kaufer, Katrin, author. | Steponaitis, Lillian K. (Lillian Kazimiera), author.
Title: Just money : mission-driven banks and the future of finance / Katrin Kaufer and Lillian Steponaitis.
Description: Cambridge, Massachusetts : The MIT Press, [2021] | Includes bibliographical references and index.
Identifiers: LCCN 2020008514 | ISBN 9780262542227 (paperback)
Subjects: LCSH: Financial institutions--Social aspects. | Banks and banking--Social aspects. | Social responsibility of business. | Social change.
Classification: LCC HG173 .K363 2021 | DDC 332.1--dc23
LC record available at https://lccn.loc.gov/2020008514

10   9   8   7   6   5   4   3   2   1

To COS
To my parents

Contents

Introduction

Banks define our future. Every investment decision writes the story of what our future will look like. This book provides an introduction to banks and financial institutions that align the impact of these decisions with the well-being of society and the planet. The urgency of the current disruptions, from the climate crisis to the stark social divides to the COVID-19 pandemic and its social and economic fallout, requires innovations and new solutions. As economic intermediaries, banks and financial institutions are in a unique position to identify and support these much-needed innovations; banks hold in their hands an important leverage point—namely, facilitating the flow of finance and money in the economy.

This book invites you on a journey to visit financial institutions around the world that have succeeded in using their unique role to take on urgent challenges. They are innovators on the margins of our financial system. And while the idea of mission-based banking and investing is not new—credit unions, impact investment funds, and microfinance institutions are well-known examples of "impact-aware" finance around the world—what is new is its rapidly growing popularity. Almost every large bank offers impact investment options to its clients. The world's largest financial technology (fintech) firm, Ant Financial, partnered with the United Nations Environment Program to launch a green digital financial alliance. One hundred eighty-one CEOs of large US companies signed a statement saying that companies should benefit all stakeholders—customers, employees, suppliers, communities, *and* shareholders—a departure from how the purpose of business was framed in the past. More than three thousand businesses worldwide are certified as B Corporations, businesses that are balancing purpose and profit.[1] BlackRock, the world's largest asset manager, talks about societal responsibility and has announced that it will include climate change considerations in its investment decision-making.

While this trend toward impact-awareness in finance and business is growing, and more and more corporations are stating their intent to conduct business in socially responsible ways, there is a long road between making these announcements and actually having meaningful impact. Since 2008, we have worked with banks and financial institutions that use finance as a tool for positive change. This book shares what we have learned and explores different aspects of this emerging field: how these banks operate, what practices and tools they have developed, the systemic barriers they are confronted with, how they balance impact with profitability. The financial institutions discussed here are niche players in the financial system, but as innovators they experiment with ideas and products that can benefit the rest of the sector.

As we write, the fight against the COVID-19 pandemic has revealed the vulnerability and interdependency of our current systems and has shown that our well-being as a society depends on our ability to act collectively. Overcoming these challenges requires not only government intervention but also a transformation of how we organize our economy and financial sector. We will not be able to address the disruptive challenges we face as societies if the financial sector does not leave the neutrality paradigm behind and begins to develop financial solutions for those challenges. What the cases in this book illustrate is that banking with a mission is more than adding impact indicators to profitability goals. If climate change threatens the survival of the planet, it is not enough to report some carbon reduction; it is also vital to finance effective innovations that secure our survival. If a community suffers from the effects of systemic marginalization and racism, enabling power and self-determination should be central to the design of financial products that serve that community. We are beginning to see innovations in these financial institutions that measure their success against whether they are able to address the challenge. Doing so requires a new economic logic. We call this new logic *ecosystem thinking* because it requires businesses to make decisions and consider impacts in the context of the overall system they operate in—be it the community, the region, the society, or the planet as a whole.

This new logic requires new tools and business practices that enable organizations to find leverage points for systemic change. Ecosystem thinking has implications for how a financial institution is organized and run, for ownership models, and for relationships with customers. Transparency and accountability become central features, leadership approaches change, and the dialogue with clients shifts.

Chapter 1 begins with a quick visit to some of these institutions around the world—a European bank that is rethinking transparency in banking, a Canadian credit union that offers an alternative to payday lending, and a bank in Bangladesh that provides financing to small-business clients that do not have access to loans through the traditional banking system. The chapter also introduces the concept and core principles of Just Banking: banking with impact awareness at the core of the business model.

Chapter 2 asks whether profit and mission are compatible or contradictory. Why do so many impact-driven banks eventually lose their connection to their founding mission to create a positive impact? We discuss what it takes for a business to hew to a nonfinancial impact objective; we also introduce the three anchors of a mission-focused business: governance, organization, and leadership.

Chapter 3 considers whether the Just Banking model can be scaled up and identifies systemic barriers these businesses face. This chapter also traces the history of impact innovation in finance with the goal to identify learnings and core concepts that form the foundation for how we think about mission-based finance today.

Financing with impact requires that we understand what is meant by impact. Chapter 4 discusses impact measurement tools and explains the importance of a learning infrastructure for effective impact assessment. The chapter also discusses the concept of a whole-system perspective as a core feature of impact measurement.

Just Banking institutions break with the traditional business raison d'être of profit maximization for running a business. Thus, chapter 5 introduces the concept of ecosystem finance and how to rethink the economy from an impact perspective. We close the chapter by exploring leverage points for creating an ecosystem-based financial system.

The title of this book, *Just Money*, is the name of an online course we developed and offer through MIT edX, a program of free online courses. The word "just" in the name means both "fair" and "only." These two meanings reflect characteristics we hope to see in the field of money and banking. The first meaning refers to how money is used and how part of the banking system is constructed to serve society as a whole: we need a fair system. The second meaning relates to the importance of money: it's just money—nothing more, nothing less. The economy and finance are just tools to serve human beings.

This book is written for a broad audience: for interested readers concerned about the impact of the economy on societal and environmental well-being, for students of finance, for practitioners of finance in Just Banking institutions and in mainstream banks. The book contributes to the discussion about the future of finance and the necessity of rethinking and revising the economic model in ways that address the disruptive challenges we see ourselves confronted with. We cannot solve the problems we face without a new vision for the current financial system—or without adopting the core principles and practices that will make the vision a reality.

Enjoy the read!

1
Just Money: Finance as a Tool for Change

A year ago, when we were walking the streets of Madrid looking for a place to have lunch, we opened an app on our cell phones and were able to find an organic restaurant just two blocks away. The app was designed by a financial institution, the Netherlands-based Triodos Bank, which has operations across Western Europe and finances social and green businesses and projects.[1] This app allowed us to locate all the bank's business customers in the area. Triodos Bank created the app because its business model is based on the concept of transparency. Customers choose Triodos Bank because they want to know how their money is used. As Triodos Bank sets social and ecological standards for its clients, the app allowed us to identify social and green businesses around us. With this app, and with a policy that requires the names of all business clients to be published on its website, Triodos Bank lifts the curtain between depositors and loan clients so that depositors know what their money is financing and with that knowledge are able to take responsibility for the impact of their money. This transparency also facilitates networking

and connections among Triodos Bank's clients, thereby growing the community of social and green businesses.

Let's move to a different continent and another online
tool created by a financial services institution. Vancity Credit
Union,[2] located in Vancouver, British Columbia, on the
west coast of Canada, created the Fair & Fast online loan, a
nonpredatory credit-building alternative to payday lending.[3] Payday loans have become an increasingly popular
credit option for families living paycheck to paycheck in the
United States and Canada. This unsecured loan provides a
cash advance based on the borrower's payroll and employ-
ment records. Payday loans are easy to acquire and may
have terms of no more than a few months. They are often
predatory, designed for clients who have no other alternative to bridge a short-term cash flow gap. Because the clients
are desperate for funds, the lender can charge an annual percentage rate (APR) as high as 600 percent in some cases. Clients who are not able to repay the loan on time may quickly
enter a cycle of debt in which they take out additional loans
to repay the rapidly accumulating interest.

Vancity Credit Union noticed that some of its members
were caught in this debt cycle and designed its Fair & Fast
Loan to provide a responsibly priced alternative and to help
members build their credit history. Credit union members
can receive Fair & Fast Loans of up to Can$2,500 with terms
of up to two years. The loans are considered fair because the
APR is low (19 percent as of January 1, 2020), payment terms
are flexible, the language of the contract is simple and transparent, and there are no hidden fees. Since the loan is not

evaluated based on the borrower's credit score, the barriers to borrowing are reduced. An added benefit is that, unlike payday lenders, Vancity reports to credit bureaus, meaning Fair & Fast Loans can help members boost their credit scores or build a credit history.

Now let's travel south to El Salvador and visit SAC Apoyo Integral, a microfinance bank operating primarily in that country. Microfinance describes a range of financial services such as lending, providing access to saving vehicles, and creating insurance pools for individuals and small businesses with no or limited access to mainstream banking, often because of poverty, social exclusion, or geographic exclusion. Microfinance aims to fight poverty and support clients in becoming self-sufficient. Integral was founded as a credit program by the nonprofit Salvadoran Foundation for Integral Support (Fundación Salvadoreña de Apoyo Integral, FUSAI) and has since become one of the fastest-growing microfinance institutions in Central America. This accomplishment is particularly impressive in light of the challenging socioeconomic conditions in El Salvador. After a two-decades-long civil war that ended in 1992, extreme levels of violence have persisted. The violence has made El Salvador one of the most dangerous countries in the world. There has also been a mass exodus of Salvadoran workers to the United States, and remittances from these workers make up around 17 percent of El Salvador's GDP.[4] In these conditions, Integral focuses on the segments of the Salvadoran population that are most in need of economic development and support. However, unlike many microfinance organizations, which operate primarily with a profit motive, Integral is driven by a mission to improve the overall quality of life of its clients and their communities. In addition to financial services, Integral offers technical assistance for home improvement, micro health and life insurance, and free financial and environmental education, among other programs. Integral develops long-term relationships with clients and uses quality-of-life improvements as an impact measure. Improvements should be sustainable in the long run and should be measurable not only in financial well-being but also in education, health, and living conditions.

Let's make a final stop in South Asia, where we step into a branch of BRAC Bank in Bangladesh. Sir Fazle Hasan Abed founded BRAC, one of the world's largest nongovernmental organizations (NGOs), to address urgent humanitarian challenges in Bangladesh and several other countries.[5] BRAC operates as a microfinance institution and also runs schools, health centers, crisis relief operations, and institutions of higher education. While microfinance, if done well, can be a first step toward a family in need securing an income, growing a business requires access to financial tools that go beyond microfinance. The next larger loan size is often called the "missing middle" because of the systemic gap in finance in providing these medium-sized loans.[6] Getting a loan can be a problem for small and medium-sized enterprises (SMEs) not only in Bangladesh. SMEs in Australia, Germany, the United States, and other high-income countries face the same challenge. The main reason is that this loan size is harder to standardize. It is more expensive for banks to service one hundred loans of $10,000 each than one loan of $1 million. But loans to SMEs are important for job creation and innovation in our economies and therefore are relevant to society as a whole.

In Bangladesh, Sir Abed and his team founded BRAC Bank, in part to address this challenge. BRAC Bank has become the largest provider of collateral-free loans in Bangladesh. Doing away with the requirement for collateral allows BRAC Bank to finance new and small entrepreneurs who have no credit history, which is common in an environment where small businesses rely primarily on cash transactions. BRAC Bank fills a systemic gap and addresses a structural challenge in finance.

Just Banking: From Ego-System to Ecosystem Finance

The financial institutions described here are examples of what we call "Just Banking"—they use finance as a tool to address social and environmental challenges. These banks translate the ideas and practices of a socially responsible enterprise into the financial sector. The socially responsible business model combines the entrepreneurial dynamic of a for-profit business with the objective of creating a positive social or ecological impact. To the goal of profitability these businesses add goals they believe will create a positive impact beyond their organizational boundary. By expanding the purpose of the business to include impact objectives, they use their innovative and entrepreneurial potential to proactively address societal challenges. Examples of social business can be found around the world and in all sectors, whether it is designing an ecological clothing line, producing sustainable cleaning products, or employing a workforce recruited from marginalized communities. Social businesses range from those that integrate a few socially responsible practices into their operation to those that create an entire business model driven by social impact.

This way of operating a business has many names: mission-driven business, social business, and triple bottom line (people, planet, profit), to name a few. But the common denominator is the decision to intentionally shift from a focus on just one variable, namely, profit, toward the impact the business has on the ecosystem in which it operates. We describe this intentional shift as moving from ego-system to ecosystem awareness.[7] Ecosystem awareness describes how an entrepreneur or a business makes decisions and sets objectives that advance the well-being of the ecosystem. The ecosystem of a company includes all key partners and collaborators that need to connect and collaborate differently in order to change how the system operates. An ecosystem can be the community in which the business is operating, the sector, or society as a whole. Ecosystem thinking requires actors to consider their impact on the larger ecosystem in their decisions. SAC Apoyo Integral's creation of a range of interventions in the communities the bank serves, from microloans to insurance to financial education and technical training, requires the bank to look at the impact of its operations on the community as a whole, not just on individual customers.

As our journey to financial institutions around the world illustrates, stepping into this ecosystem perspective and creating a positive impact with financial institutions requires structural innovations and changes to standard financial practice. These changes include increasing transparency, developing client-centered innovations, and putting in place new operational processes. The shift also has implications for the culture and leadership of the organization. Although this type of banking has existed for years, a growing number of financial institutions are aiming to innovate ecosystem finance practices and methods.

Banks that put positive societal impact on an equal footing with or even before profit challenge the popular image of banking. Why do these banks exist? Are they merely exceptions to the rule, or are they innovating in ways that will influence how we think about the role of banking in the future?

Banks Define Our Future

Addressing the urgent challenges of our time, such as climate change, health, and inequality, requires a host of systemic interventions. We propose that finance should be included in this discussion. In many ways, banks define our future. Tamara Vrooman, the CEO of Vancity Credit Union, summarizes the relevance of banks as follows:

> The allocation of capital is one of the strongest determinants of the future society that we create. Who gets a loan, who doesn't, who gets equity, who doesn't, really determines

the kind of future we're creating. We need to think about how we allocate capital in the context of the current climate crisis, and we need to act quickly. This is an emergency that won't be fixed by bailouts and interest rate tweaks. But it can be effectively addressed by sustainable finance. Today, financial institutions number among the world's largest companies; our sector has an enormous economic and political footprint. We should be rallying that influence by developing new partnerships, rethinking old business models, and redefining some of the assumptions that lie at the foundations of our economy.[8]

Every business has an impact on societal well-being, whether it is a positive impact, such as the provision of goods and services, or a negative impact, such as environmental pollution. But as intermediaries, banks play a unique role in the structure of an economic system, and therefore the impact of their decisions is magnified.

Banks facilitate financial transactions, a service that every actor in the economy depends on. Banks' role as intermediaries and the fact that they deal with money make them different from any other business. Access to financial services is the entry card to the economy, and banks and financial institutions are the gatekeepers. If banking fails, economies collapse. And as Tamara Vrooman suggests, this is why banks get rescued by governments and by taxpayers.

Combining banking with a mission is not a recent innovation. Credit unions, which are cooperative financial institutions owned by the members they serve, began operating in Germany and England in the nineteenth century.[9] The foundational idea of credit unions was to help members, usually from low-income or marginalized communities, save money and gain access affordable loans. This concept spread through Europe and arrived in the United States at the beginning of the twentieth century. Socially responsible businesses, which combine an emphasis on societal impact with a for-profit business model, also are not new. These businesses have become popular in many parts of the world over the past thirty years. And in finance we have seen a rise in the popularity of socially responsible and impact investment.

In the aftermath of the global financial crisis of 2007–2009, the public debate over the role and responsibility of banks changed. Since banks were rescued using taxpayer money, the question of their accountability to the rest of society has been posed prominently. A heated topic was the revolving door between bankers and government officials; another was the financial deregulation of the 1980s and 1990s, especially the 1999 repeal of the Glass-Steagall Act in the United States. The Glass-Steagall Act was written into law in 1933 to restore confidence in the banking sector after the financial crisis of 1929. A core element of the act was the separation of commercial banking from investment banking, with the aim of protecting banking from the more high-risk investment banking activities. Another essential part of the act was the creation of the Federal Deposit Insurance Corporation (FDIC), which provides deposit insurance to depositors in the United States.[10] As the debate continues over whether and how to regulate institutions in ways that protect consumers and reinforce the unique responsibility banks carry, banks and policymakers have slowly begun to change their rhetoric and approach. For example, the European Commission published an action plan for sustainable finance in 2018 that includes a regulatory proposal to support sustainable investment.[11]

Finance and Money—the Access Cards to Our Economy

Access to financial services is the entry card to the economic system, and without access, consumers and entrepreneurs cannot fully participate in it. We find underbanked and unbanked communities and individuals in most regions of the world. A 2017 survey by the FDIC concluded that 25 percent of Americans are unbanked or underbanked, meaning they have no or limited access to financial services.[12] Globally, 30 percent of all adults are unbanked or underbanked.[13]

There are many reasons why people have limited or no access to banking services. For example, the costs of maintaining and running a brick-and-mortar branch in sparsely populated rural areas might be too high for the bank to be profitable. But racial or ethnic discrimination can also limit access to financial services. A well-documented example in the United States is the practice of redlining. In 1935 the US Federal Home Loan Bank Board drew lines around particular neighborhoods on maps and shared these maps with banks. Redlined neighborhoods were considered more financially risky than bluelined neighborhoods. Those lines were often drawn based on the racial makeup of the neighborhoods and created a self-fulfilling prophecy. Residents of redlined neighborhoods could not access credit in the form of a mortgage or a loan to start or expand a business, regardless of their actual creditworthiness. This practice helped create a vicious cycle of disinvestment in minority neighborhoods in many US cities and opened the door for predatory lenders to fill the void.[14] Though redlining has been illegal since the 1970s, the practice created long-term damage to the economic outcomes of communities of color in the United States that can still be seen to this day. This is one prominent example, but financial discrimination based on race, ethnicity, or immigration status is pervasive around the globe, limiting economic access and with that, opportunities to build wealth, power, and well-being.[15]

Banks' decisions as to what to fund, where to invest, and whom to serve have ripple effects that extend far beyond the economic realm. Thomas Jorberg, the CEO of GLS Bank in Germany, one of the earliest social and green banks in Europe, summarized this in reflecting on his early experience as a banker:

> One of the first things I learned when I began my training as a banker was from one of my mentors. I will never forget this. He said, "a loan can destroy a life, and a loan can save a life." I then realized banking is about humans taking responsibility for what is happening with their money and what their money gets invested in.[16]

The criteria banks include in their decision-making processes matter, not just to the bank but to society overall.

Just Banking: Using Finance as a Tool to Address Societal Issues

What we call "impact" can come in many forms—poverty reduction; reducing carbon emissions; increasing affordable housing stock; growing local, sustainable food systems; providing banking services for underserved communities. The principles of Just Banking that are outlined in this book are part of a growing movement among businesses that combines financial profitability with social or environmental impact, or both.

Says CEO Jorberg of GLS Bank:

> The founding idea [for GLS Bank] that was developed at the end of the '60s was to use and invest money in a way that initiates positive social, ecological, and cultural developments in our society. The founding idea really was to use money to shape society. You can use money in a conscious way to shape society in a social and ecological way. A lot of people want this today, and we invest their money in a way that they know they're financing an educational project, or regenerative energy, or an organic farm. I can connect my intention, my ideals, and my ideas with the way I invest my money and with that I can shape society.[17]

This form of finance fits our definition of Just Money—money being used in a responsible manner to support the activities of the real economy and aim for a positive impact on the ecosystem the institution serves.

How Is Just Banking Different?

All banks weigh nonfinancial risk assessment criteria when making an investment decision, but Just Banking makes the impact analysis central. Says Peter Blom, CEO of Triodos Bank : "Our first priority is to have impact."[18]

Triodos Bank describes impact as follows:

> Having the power to transform, directing money so that it benefits people and the environment over the long-term. Our vision on measuring impact reflects a focus on delivering our mission. That means we try and find qualitative evidence of the impact first and foremost and back it up with numbers when it's relevant.[19]

Financial institutions have different options for integrating impact assessment into the financial decision-making process: they can be reactive, proactive, or both.

1. *Reactive:* Banks create policies and structures to protect their investments from social and ecological risks or in response to changing public opinion or regulations. Climate risks might cause banks to pull out of investments that contribute to climate change, such as coal mining. However, they must consider whether divestment could hurt their brand, or whether proposed regulations could cause them to revisit their decision.

Amy Domini, a pioneer of the socially responsible investment movement, describes how she began to integrate impact into investment decisions:

In 1975 I started working as a retail stockbroker in Cambridge, Massachusetts. That job description doesn't exist anymore....Each morning at 9 o'clock we listened to a squawk box, which would announce, "We think that this particular company is an excellent buy right now. Here's the reason." If you liked the reason, you would call your clients and say, "We think this is an excellent company to buy right now, and here's the reason."

I found myself occasionally getting pushback from clients for unexpected reasons....They would say to me, "They make weapons, don't they? No. I'm not interested in owning part of a weapons manufacturer." Or they would say, "Aren't they a paper company? You do know I'm the head of the local Audubon Society and I spend all my free time fighting paper companies and the dioxin they spray on forests." I began to realize that it was hard enough to find a client who wants to take your phone call. I didn't want to be introducing ideas they found offensive. So, I started taking a new approach during the getting-to-know-you stage. When first meeting a new client I began to ask if there were areas that they would rather not hear about investing in. The result was remarkable.

When the question was posed, virtually everybody said "Yeah, I suppose I wouldn't want to invest in something that actually hurts children." Virtually everyone would draw the line at something. That got me thinking that I really needed to understand this aspect of the investment process. It's easy enough to listen to an announcement that such-and-such a company has a great shot of going up. It's a lot harder to know whether or not the client is inclined toward that idea. People tend to come to the field of what I've since then called "ethical investing," because of a desire to not be in conflict with themselves, hopefully to become confluent with themselves in the investment process.[20]

The socially responsible investment movement, also known as the impact investment movement, was launched in the late

1970s and early 1980s, and has grown ever since. It began by excluding specific investments that were not aligned with the objectives of the investor. Some banks describe this reactive step of excluding investments as "minimum criteria." For example, Triodos Bank excludes investments in gambling, nuclear power, weapons, genetic engineering, and factory farming. Process-related exclusions include violations of labor or human rights, and corruption. On its website, Triodos Bank also posts position papers on specific subjects, such as animal testing, human rights, and renewable energy. These position papers summarize the current thinking in Triodos Bank on different topics and inform both internal stakeholders such as loan officers and external clients of Triodos Bank's position on a wide range of topics.[21]

But reactive exclusion alone does not necessarily have the positive impact needed to address all challenges and issues. Banks also take proactive steps.

2. *Proactive:* Positive investment criteria aim to actively create impact. Some financial institutions were founded with the purpose of generating a positive impact on a community or a specific group. Says Matthijs Bierman, director of the Triodos Bank branch in the Netherlands: "Triodos Bank's competitors have a banking model that is very different. They mostly avoid the wrong kind of investments, so they have a lot of exclusionary criteria. Whereas we deal with much more positive criteria, we deliberately seek out those activities which drive positive change."[22]

The main challenge of this proactive approach is understanding the impact of an investment decision. We dive into this question in chapter 4. With both approaches, reactive and proactive, the financial sector is participating in a trend that has engaged the rest of the corporate world for some time. Entities that operate with the double or triple bottom line in mind (people, planet, profit), such as B Corporations—businesses certified according to their social and environmental impact—and social or green businesses, can be found around the world. What all these businesses have in common is a simple innovation: directing entrepreneurial energy toward disruptive solutions to societal challenges. What they all struggle with is understanding the complexity of assessing and expanding the societal impact they are aiming for.

Where Does Your Money Sleep at Night? Principles of Just Banking

We have learned in our work with Just Banking institutions and social entrepreneurs that combining profitability with a mission requires a different set of tools, methods, and practices from those used in mainstream banking. Including quantitative objectives in day-to-day operations changes how a business is organized and how it assesses its success. The first step in Just Banking is to ask what impact the investment will have on society.

Tina Narron, chief lending officer for Verity Credit Union, a midsized credit union in Seattle, Washington, that is shifting its corporate strategy toward Just Banking, shared this anecdote in one of our conversations:

> Last month we declined a financially solid loan application
> for the first time because of impact reasons. That was new
> for us. We told the customer: "You will easily find a bank
> that will fund this development. From a financial point
> of view this is a solid project. But the project will displace
> tenants, and because of that we are not able to fund you."
> The customer accepted this. This was a strange experience
> for us, but we were all aligned here.[23]

This decision illustrates the core idea of Just Banking. Understanding the impact of a loan is central to decision-making. The lender is required to introduce transparency into a decision and to dig deeper into the potential impact of making a loan.

Here is an example provided by Patty Zuidhoek, director of business banking for Triodos Bank in the Netherlands:

> Although we are proud to help finance the energy transition
> and believe we need a lot of renewable energy, and solar
> is one of our key sectors, we decided not to finance [a]
> large quantity of solar panels on the roof of an industrial
> operating farm because this nonorganic farmer wanted to
> reduce his energy costs [in order] to have money to hold
> more pigs in his farm and expand the number of intensively
> held animals. We had no agreement on a mission level
> about animal well-being, diversity, usage of chemicals, etc.
> with the farmer. If the farmer would have wanted to change
> his farm to organic, we would have done the financing of
> the solar panels.[24]

Over time, Triodos Bank has developed position papers on the different fields in which it operates, such as agriculture and renewable energy. Patty Zuidhoek uses this background research to assess the loan applications she receives: yes, increasing renewable energy is crucial to address climate change, but no, industrial agriculture is not acceptable. Which of these two elements in the loan application is more important?

Just Banking institutions have developed different processes to help them respond to this assessment challenge. Solutions range from applying exclusion and inclusion criteria to innovating the process of assessing a loan application. An exceptional example of this comes from Banca Popolare Etica, a cooperative bank in Italy. The bank's members are also owners of the bank. Banca Popolare Etica trains some of its members to participate in the impact assessment of a potential business loan. The loan cannot go forward without the approval of the member reviewer.

The following core principles summarize what we have learned from a decade of work with Just Banking institutions:

Principle 1: Just Banks Use Finance as a Tool to Address Societal Challenges

This first principle is about intentionality. "Neutrality is a lack of responsibility" is the way Pierre Aeby, the longtime CFO of Triodos Bank, describes his philosophy.[25] Just Banking is not a neutral approach to banking; it takes a position by asking, is this investment good for society or not? Understanding the impact of a loan decision might not always be clear-cut and easy, but asking the question is the starting point for Just Banking.

Societies today are faced with disruptive challenges on a global scale, including climate change, the COVID-19 pandemic, inequality, and refugee crises. Regulatory responses to these challenges are effective but reactive, meaning they address the challenges once those challenges receive enough attention—for example, attention from stakeholders such as NGOs that push for CO_2 emission goals, or from advocates for refugees. Also, new regulations take time to put in place. Social entrepreneurship aims to take a proactive approach by directing innovative and dynamic capacity toward societal challenges. Fairphone in Europe is developing a socially and ecologically responsive cell phone whose materials are sourced in a responsible way, including the working conditions for miners, and is designed so that it can be taken apart and be repaired. The clothing retailers Patagonia and Eileen Fisher are producing socially and ecologically responsible clothing lines and experimenting with circular economy processes—for example, by developing supply chains that seek to eliminate waste, reuse materials, and minimize the use of scarce resources. Eileen Fisher will take back gently worn clothes from customers and resell them. Patagonia encourages repair of its products and even offers a repair service.[26]

This core principle of Just Banking is about recognizing the unique role financial institutions play in society and leveraging that role to create positive social impacts.

Principle 2: Just Banking Is at the Core of the Business Model

Most banks have a corporate social responsibility (CSR) department or social or green portfolios that are add-ons to their main business operation. What distinguishes Just Banking is that the mission and impact objectives are at the core

of the business model. The mission is not part of a branding campaign but is where the business generates its profits.
Says Peter Blom of Triodos Bank, "Our customers come to us
because they want to make sure their money is doing good in
the world. Losing their trust is the biggest risk of our business
model."[27]

This business model requires decision-makers to step
outside the boundaries of their organization and add impact
analysis to the financial review of every investment decision. The quantitative objective of profitability is joined
to an expanded qualitative review of impact. The task of
balancing these two assessments reaches into every part of
the organization: the leadership, the compensation policy,
relationships with customers, risk analysis, and the communication strategy. In our work with Just Bankers, we often
hear that they need to reinvent the conventional tools of
banking from an impact perspective

In an impact-driven business model, a qualitative impact
analysis of any business decision is integrated into daily
practice. Every bank or financial institution includes qualitative criteria in its decision-making process, but mostly from
a risk-analysis perspective. Just Banking conducts this qualitative analysis to determine whether and how investments
will improve the social and ecological well-being of society.
This requires an intentional shift toward ecosystem thinking,
stepping into the perspective of the ecosystem in which the
bank operates.

This is easier said than done, and we delve into the different forms of impact analysis in a later chapter. Briefly,

however, what we have seen in mission-driven banks over the past decade is that operating according to a double or triple bottom line leads to financial innovations that differentiate these institutions in the market, such as the Vancity Fair & Fast Loan or the Triodos app mentioned earlier. It also requires new ways of operating, through innovations in leadership, processes, and organizational structures.

Principle 3: Just Banking Is an Activity: Aligning the What, How, and Why

No bank operates as a Just Bank 100 percent of the time. Even the greenest and most socially responsible bank is required to park some of its cash reserves with its national central bank. In that moment, the bank loses control over what its funds are invested in. So, Just Banking is not maintaining a status quo; it is an *activity*. Banks engage in Just Banking when they use finance as a tool for social change.

An easy way to identify Just Banking practices in the financial sector is to ask three questions: What, how, and why.

1. *What:* This is the question about impact. What is the outcome of the banking activity? The app that guided the search for an organic restaurant in Madrid was developed by Triodos Bank to make the "what" very transparent: customers know exactly what their money finances.

2. *How:* How does the bank operate? Does the bank pay a living wage?[28] How does the bank treat its customers? Is it inclusive? The "how" dives into the operation and structure of the bank.

3. *Why:* Why does the bank do what it does? One way to answer this question is to look at the ownership structure of the bank. Who is holding the capital, and with what intention? Are owners looking for a quick return or are they aligned with the long-term intention of the bank?

Because we define Just Banking as an activity, these questions can be applied not just to the banks but also to the companies and individuals they choose to invest in. Let's apply these three steps to an example. I am concerned about climate change and want my money to be invested in renewable energy. I identify an opportunity to invest in a wind farm. That is the "what." The result of my investment is the production of renewable energy. Next I ask "how." Where is the wind farm located, and how will its operation affect the local community and the nearby environment? How will the wind farm be managed? Will the workers be paid a living wage? If not, what compromises can I accept and still consider this a socially responsible investment? Will the communities near the wind farm benefit in any way from the construction? Finally, I ask "why." Why is this wind farm being constructed? Who will reap the profits? Who will own it, and what are the intentions of the owner: to maximize profit at all costs or to balance profit and impacts on society?

As one coworker in a mission-driven bank told us, "In my old job, I always knew what the target was: maximizing profit. Now my work is so much more complex. I have to review every step on the way, and it is much more difficult to understand when I fulfill expectations."[29]

Principle 4: Just Banking Balances Standardization with Context Awareness

The more a bank standardizes its business, the lower its costs, and thus the higher its profits if all other factors remain constant. This principle applies to all businesses, but to banks especially. Why? The more a bank standardizes its products, the less attention it needs to pay to the context of an investment and the lower its operating costs.

Standardization increases efficiency in an organization. But standardization disconnects the bank from understanding and responding to the local and differentiated needs of clients and communities. Finding the right balance of these opposing goals is the art of Just Banking.

This challenge of balancing standardization with the context is old news. The Community Reinvestment Act (CRA), which encourages regulated financial institutions to invest in local communities, became law in the United States in 1977 and was given teeth by the Clinton administration in the 1990s through increased reporting standards and enforcement. The CRA was an attempt to counterbalance the tendency of US banks to disconnect from context and under-invest in low- and middle-income communities.

While investors are often pulled toward large national and international projects and business opportunities, SMEs at the local level can struggle to access loans. As we described earlier with the example of BRAC Bank, this missing middle is a structural issue in banking that mirrors how the interests of a bank and societal needs can be misaligned and how the pull of standardization can create systemic deficiencies—for example, when banks standardize their business loans and new and small businesses or innovative new initiatives don't fit into the standardized assessment scheme.

This fourth principle is a challenging one for Just Banking. It requires a bank to develop and integrate operational policies and structures that allow it to balance these two opposing objectives: connecting to the specific context of an investment and standardizing an effective operation.

Principle 5: Just Banking Requires Transparency and Accountability

A business model that uses finance to address societal challenges creates opportunities for the bank to connect its customers to the impact it is creating. Consequently, transparency is central to the success of Just Banking. Several banks in Europe that operate on Just Banking principles require all their business clients to agree that their names will be made public. At the beginning of the chapter we described the Triodos Bank app that allows anyone to find Triodos customers on an interactive map. GLS Bank in Germany, Merkur Bank in Denmark, and ABS in Switzerland do the same: every business loan is published on the website, on an app, or in the bank's customer magazine.

This level of transparency lifts the curtain between the depositors and the creditors and in doing so answers the question, What does your money finance? This transparency also increases the level of accountability between the bank and its clients. Customers have access to data about what their money finances and are invited to ask questions and provide feedback about the funded projects. This level of transparency makes banks accountable for what they fund, but it also increases the reputational risks: that is, if customers find the bank is making investments they don't like or they believe do not fit with the bank's mission, they may choose to pull their money out of the bank.

MIT's Simon Johnson, a coauthor of *13 Bankers: The Wall Street Takeover and the Next Financial Meltdown*,[30] sees transparency and accountability as core features of banks in the future, and argues that the digitization of the financial sector will advance this trend:

> I believe we will see in the future of banking much more transparency, much more accountability, much more visibility so you can see what not just banks, but other companies are doing. This is what we're going to get with the decentralized set of technologies that are loosely referred to as blockchain. You're going to have a lot more visibility of who did what and when. Intermediaries like banks are going to have to choose how much they show to different stakeholders.[31]

Transparency requires banks to invite their stakeholders into a dialogue about impact and objectives. At the end of the day, impact-driven banks are accountable to the communities they serve. The task they face is how best to create accountability processes that balance effectiveness, entrepreneurial opportunity, and impact. Some of these processes are more tangible than others. A governance structure anchors accountability to shareholders and members of the business. Annual impact reports, for example, are tangible forms of accountability to stakeholders. But the bank might also integrate less tangible forms of accountability into how it operates that helps it stay connected to its mission. When you sit in a meeting room in Triodos Bank you will see one red and one green chair among the black chairs around the conference table. The green chair is a reminder to consider the future of the planet at each meeting; the red chair is a reminder that your decisions will affect the future of the community. Operating with impact requires paying attention to the voices of those who have no seat at the table when decisions are made.

Just Banking: Innovation at the Margins

These five principles distinguish Just Banking practices and explain how this form of banking and finance differs from the mainstream financial sector. Just Banking involves our human capacity to assess, innovate, and be entrepreneurial, and it requires the skills to step into an ecosystem perspective. Ecosystem thinking is the intentional assessment of a decision from a system perspective and an exploration of the negative and positive impacts of a decision from this perspective.

Just Banking occupies a small niche in the financial sector. But as the mainstream discussion begins to question the role, function, and impact of banks, this book asks whether these niche players can provide lessons and insights that are valuable for the sector as a whole. The following chapters explore practices, tools, and ideas that these innovators have developed and tested. They also ask whether these innovations are marginal or whether they can be scaled up for the benefit of the entire financial sector.

2
The Anchoring Triangle: Rethinking Governance, Organization, and Leadership

The history of Just Banking businesses shows that the intention to create positive change in society is an objective that can easily be lost or watered down. Even when they are founded with a mission to create positive change in society, businesses do not always succeed in keeping this mission alive over the long run.

An example here concerns a small public bank owned by a municipality in Germany. When the city of Berlin, Germany, like so many cities around the world, began to see a speculative shift in its real estate market after 2014, some investors jumped on the opportunity to profit from rising demand and began buying and flipping real estate, often displacing long-term residents. One of these speculative investors was funded by a mission-based bank in southern Germany, a *Sparkasse* (savings bank). The explicit mission of the bank is to operate regionally, so why would a bank owned by a municipality four hundred miles from Berlin speculate in this heated market? It seems that the pull of high profit margins won out over mission and purpose.[1]

As action researchers, we have worked with banks that have followed Just Banking principles for decades, as well as with banks that have only recently decided to shift toward operating according to Just Banking principles.[2] What we have learned in our research is that successfully combining profitability with a mission requires an "anchoring of the mission" in the organization. There are three core anchors: governance, organizational structure, and leadership.

Is There a Trade-off between Profit and Mission?

One frequently asked question about Just Banking is whether there is a trade-off between profitability and the mission to create a positive social impact. The few studies that compare mission-driven businesses with conventional businesses have concluded that the impact of the mission-driven operation on profitability varies, which is not surprising.[3] Business profitability depends on many factors, including the maturity of the markets, the competition, and organizational efficiency. It is difficult to isolate the impact of a mission objective from that of the rest of a business's operations.

A different response to whether profit and mission compete comes from Pierre Aeby, former CFO at Triodos Bank. He argues that the role of profit changes in a mission-driven organization, and that this applies not only to Just Banking but also to any social business or social enterprise that operates with double- or triple-bottom-line objectives (people, planet, profit). "Profit is not the goal, but rather an indicator of whether we are successful. Our objective is not to maximize our profit but to create a fair profit that allows the business to operate in the long run."[4]

Aeby thinks about profit from an impact perspective, which requires an intentional shift toward ecosystem thinking. The overall purpose of his organization is to achieve impact; consequently, profit becomes one among several objectives that support this overall purpose. Most important, profit enables the business to operate and to increase impact; without profit, the bank would close. And second, profitability serves as an indicator of the level of organizational efficiency. In this view, profit is a means to an end, not an end in itself.

The shift from profit as the main objective of the business to profit as an indicator is not a technical change. Profit is still calculated in the same way, but seeing profit as one goal among others requires an intentional shift. Redefining profit has a very real and tangible impact on how a business is run—for example, how the organization is led, what kinds of products and services the business provides, and how success is measured. This shift affects all areas of the business and must be intentionally incorporated into everything from lending practices to key performance indicators. For example, a loan review committee must consider the social and environmental impact of prospective borrowers' use for the funds. When transparency is core to the business model—that is, when a bank wants its customers to know what their money is underwriting—the communications and marketing departments need to incorporate this objective into their strategy.

It is this balancing of several objectives that differentiates Just Banking institutions from conventional banks. Just Banking requires operating from what we call an "ecosystem perspective," which describes decision-making from a perspective that explores the negative and positive impacts of a decision on the whole system. Operationally, ecosystem thinking requires a bank to (1) develop new organizational practices and processes that reflect the business's impact on its ecosystem and (2) design a business operation that is capable of pursuing the various relevant and sometimes competing business objectives.

The increased complexity of operating according to Just Banking principles also comes with opportunities to innovate and enter new markets. In the 1980s, Netherlands-based Triodos Bank and Germany's GLS Bank were the first banks in Europe to develop financial products that enabled investments in wind energy, a market that is well established today. After the global financial crisis of 2007–2009, Just Banking institutions saw an unprecedented increase in customers.

Moving beyond profit or shareholder value maximization as the sole business objective is an emerging field. But the pressing challenges of our time, from the climate crisis to inequality and public health, are pushing the diversification of business objectives into the strategy decisions of more and more companies, which acknowledge that their impact on society is a variable they need to consider in order to succeed. The moment a business begins to integrate social impact objectives into its operations, the question of how to implement this shift arises. How does the relationship between the customer and the loan officer change if the loan officer receives a bonus? How does an organization develop a compensation scheme that reflects its values as a socially responsible business and create the working conditions for integrating the mission objectives into the organization?

When maximizing profit and shareholder value is no longer the only variable determining the success of the organization, the complexity of how to define success increases. The intentional shift toward aiming for a positive impact on the ecosystem the bank operates in requires a broadening of the assessment process and an alignment of the operational functions. The organization needs to adapt and innovate in ways that integrate all objectives, even when they compete with one another.

Institutional Anchoring of Just Banking Principles

When we present Just Banking to students, we usually get two reactions. The first is surprise that Just Banking exists. The second is the expectation that banks following these principles will lose or reduce their impact focus over the long run. There is some truth to that, for Just Banking institutions must balance several, sometimes competing, objectives.

Successful impact-focused banks anchor their values and mission at different levels of the organization and its operations. "Anchoring" means these banks create practices, policies, and structures that support the impact objectives and connect them to day-to-day operations. For example, a loan assessment by GLS Bank in Germany has two steps: the financial assessment and the impact assessment. Only if a loan application passes both steps is it approved. Banca Popolare Etica, a cooperative bank in Italy, developed a new loan assessment process that includes the bank's own members in evaluating the impact of a loan. The financial assessment is done by the bank, but Banca Popolare Etica trains volunteers from its member base to conduct an impact assessment of loan applications. If a proposed project fails the impact assessment, even if it is financially strong, the loan does not go forward.

Another loan innovation practice from an impact perspective is requiring all business loan recipients to agree that their names will be made public, as Triodos Bank does. This practice ensures full transparency. Customers can see what their deposits finance, and they become part of a community of people who share the same intent: to put their money where their ideals and ideas for the future lie.

These are some examples of how the impact objective changes the operation of a Just Banking institution. In a for-profit organization, anchoring a mission requires reinventing some of the core operations and structures. The anchoring triangle shows the three important anchors (see figure 2.1).

Governance

The governance model of a company defines the legal structure of the organization—the ownership model and the

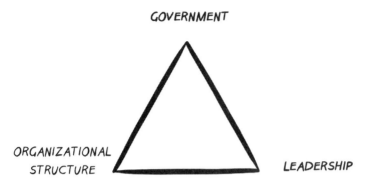

Figure 2.1
Anchoring triangle of Just Banking

decision-making bodies—and with that puts core procedures for oversight and accountability in place.[5] The governance structure has critical implications for the business model, the overarching strategy, and day-to-day operations.

Designing the right governance structure is a challenge not just for mission-based businesses. One example that illustrates the relevance and complexity of the governance question is the recent trend, especially in high-tech and family businesses, to introduce dual-class shares when going public. The share class offered to the general public comes with limited or no voting rights, while the share class available to founders and executives comes with more voting power. The purpose of having two types of shares is usually to ensure that the founders or family retain control of the company. Well-known businesses that use dual-class shares include Facebook, Alibaba, LinkedIn, and Snap Inc. In Facebook's two-tier voting structure, class A shareholders have one vote per share; class B shareholders, who comprise Facebook's management and directors, have ten votes per share. Founder and current chairman Mark Zuckerberg controls 58 percent of the company's vote because he holds 75 percent of Facebook's class B shares. Attempts by external shareholders to limit Zuckerberg's power, especially in the wake of criticism of Facebook's faulty privacy policy and data breaches, have failed because Zuckerberg controls the votes.

Snap Inc., the camera and social media company that produces Snapchat, stepped into the extreme end of this trend when its initial $3.4 billion public offering in 2017 gave investors zero voting rights. Hong Kong's stock exchange lost out to the New York Stock Exchange for Alibaba Group Holding Ltd.'s record $25 billion listing in 2014. Alibaba chose the New York Stock Exchange so that it could create a dual-class share system, which Hong Kong did not allow at the time. In 2018, Hong Kong changed its regulation, as did Singapore, and UK regulators are considering allowing dual-class shares in the future. Dual-class shares were mostly banned on US stock markets before the 1980s, with some exceptions, such as when Ford Motor Company was listed in 1956.[6] Since then, more stock exchanges worldwide have introduced dual-class shares. One-fifth of companies listed on US stock exchanges in 2017 had dual-class shares,[7] but the debate over whether they should be allowed continues.[8]

The separation of voting rights from financial returns reflects a core conflict between the intention of a founder or owners of a company and its investors. While investors criticize voting restrictions for being undemocratic and limiting governance oversight, the founders of the company or the family that owns the business argue that dual-class voting rights protect their businesses from outside interests. Questions about the legality and undemocratic nature of the two-class shareholder system are valid, but we believe they miss an essential point.

The conflict between founders and shareholders might be a power play, but it is more than that. The example of dual-class voting rights points to our earlier discussion of balancing profit maximization with other business objectives. The renewed interest in the two-class shareholder model reflects this dilemma. Investors with a strong focus on profit may be driven by short-term interests, but a thriving business needs to innovate, make hard decisions in times of change, and have the courage to step into new markets; some of these actions might compete with a profit-maximizing goal, especially when profitability is measured over the short term. The founder's ideas and long-term vision for the business may call for smaller returns. This is not to say that all investors are impatient and don't support long-term strategies that negatively affect short-term returns. It is to say that the question of who makes the judgments and decisions about corporate strategy is central to this debate.

This brings us to the question of what governance structure best allows organizations to balance profitability and other, potentially competing, objectives.[9] All the Just Banking institutions we have worked with operate with governance models that anchor the mission through their ownership structure. We consider a mission-aligned governance model a minimum condition for Just Banking—minimum because it is a necessary but not sufficient condition to ensure success-ful operation over the long run.

Examples of Ownership Models in Just Banking Businesses

Just Banks take different approaches to anchoring a mission in the governance model. Here we return to Triodos Bank in Europe for an example.

Instead of issuing shares, Triodos Bank issues depository receipts in a trust that owns the bank's share capital. Trad-ing of these receipts doesn't take place on a stock market but is organized by Triodos Bank itself. The voting rights are held by an independent legal entity, the Foundation for the Administration of Triodos Bank Shares (SAAT). Albert Hollander, group legal and compliance officer at Triodos, explains: "Our shares are certified, so that the voting rights are with a foundation, SAAT. The board of SAAT consists of independent individuals that guard the mission of Triodos. We're not listed on the stock exchange. We do trade our depository receipts publicly on an internal market."[10]

The main difference between the Triodos Bank shareholder system and the two-class shareholder system that Facebook, Alibaba, and Snap Inc. use is that a foundation replaces the founder or a family. The foundation is tasked to bridge and "align the economic interests of its depository receipt hold-ers and Triodos Bank's mission, for their mutual benefit."[11] The daily management of Triodos Bank lies with the executive board.

At their annual meeting the holders of the depository receipts vote on the appointment of the members of the board of SAAT. The board members themselves recommend candidates to join the board. These recommendations must be approved by Triodos Bank's management board and supervisory board. No depository receipt holder may hold more than 10 percent of all depository receipts issued, which prevents a hostile takeover. Says Triodos former CFO Pierre Aeby, "I think we have a quite special model in the field of alternative banks. We have most of our capital placed with our customers. More than ninety percent of our capital is owned by a very broad public, so with people strongly committed to our values who don't sell easily our shares. During our 30 years of operation, we have shown that it can work."[12]

This ownership structure is intended to ensure that in the long run, Triodos Bank balances its diverse objectives and does not move away from its mission. The founders of Triodos Bank believed that this ownership model would allow for a dialogue on the bank's direction and development between those who benefit financially from the bank and those who are primarily interested in its mission and impact. The major disadvantage of this model is its complexity. Its advantage is that the model anchors the mission and protects the bank from a hostile takeover.

Like Triodos Bank, a majority of financial institutions that operate according to Just Banking principles have governance models that serve as institutional anchors of the mission. Another example is GLS Bank in Germany, a cooperative owned by its members. A general membership assembly elects six members of the board; the remaining three are elected by the coworkers of the company. At BRAC Bank in

Bangladesh, a privately held commercial bank, 50 percent of its shares are owned by mission-aligned organizations. Southern Bancorp in the United States operates a bank and a nonprofit, both of which support development in its communities and are connected through a holding company. Table 2.1 provides a snapshot of the different governance structures of mission-driven banks.

Deciding on an Ownership Model

City First Bank of Washington, D.C., is a community development bank founded to provide more equitable access to finance for underserved low-income and minority communities. Its CEO, Brian Argrett, describes the founding of the bank and its ownership model as follows:

> The way City First was founded completely impacts and sets the course for what we do today. What's unusual about the bank is that it really came out of activism, out of community engagement. It was founded by individuals who saw, in Washington, DC, that there were neighborhoods where capital was not flowing, where there has been large-scale disinvestment, where really the banking community was not interested. And they came together to fashion a solution for how to assist in having capital flow. They chose the banking model because of the benefits of leverage through deposits. They could raise a certain amount of capital, and then they could also raise additional funds through deposits and have a larger impact in their lending. What they did, though, was they formed a nonprofit to really be the control shareholder, the founder of the bank. And to this day, that nonprofit is the largest single owner of the bank. It has voting control of the bank. And then they

Table 2.1
Examples of ownership and governance in Just Banking models

Name	Focus	Ownership form	Governance	Intention
GLS Bank, Germany	Social and ecological projects exclusively	Cooperative with 52,000 members (in 2019) and 220,000 customers	• General membership assembly • Board with 9 members (6 elected by the general assembly, 3 by coworkers)	To give members and coworkers a voice and create a community that takes responsibility for its money
BRAC Bank, Bangladesh	Small and medium-sized enterprises; social responsibility	Private commercial bank with 50% of shares held by mission-aligned organizations[13]	• Board of directors • Management committee	To ensure that the bank serves the underbanked
Southern Bancorp, USA	Rural and underserved communities	Southern Bancorp, Inc., a bank holding company of Southern Bancorp Bank, and Southern Bancorp, a nonprofit	• Governance board for each entity	To provide communities with two types of money: "gift" money, which is not expected to provide a return, and loans and financial services, which operate according to for-profit principles
Triodos Bank, Europe	Social, cultural, and ecological projects exclusively	Foundation holds shares and voting rights; depository holders receive profits; restrictions on institutional investors	• Boards for each entity • Depository holders elect the foundation board	To create an ongoing dialogue on mission, fair return, and accountability

sold shares to other investors, who also share that vision.
So what does that mean on the ground? It means that [at]
the heart of this for-profit bank in Washington, City First
Bank of DC, we really have the history, and the essence I
say, [of] a nonprofit spirit [that] kind of flows through our
veins. So, there's really a sense of wanting to, and needing
to, and being put here to really benefit those underlying
communities.[14]

Argrett illustrates the connection between the founding
process and anchoring the intention and mission of the
bank in the ownership model. He also describes how relevant this anchoring of the mission is for operating the bank
today. The founders succeeded in ensuring that the bank
stays accountable to the community it serves by anchoring
the community's interests in the governance structure. The
mission becomes part of the "DNA" of the organization.

Stepping back, we see that at the core of this decision on
an ownership model is a tension between private ownership
and public interest. This tension has long been reflected in
the debate over what legitimizes ownership. Consider, for
example, the German constitution, which states, "The ownership of property comes with responsibility."[15] The con-
temporary political scientist Manfred Brocker analyzes this
tension when he identifies a paradigm shift in our thinking about property from early "occupation theory" to John
Locke's "natural law" of ownership through exertion of
labor. Locke, a seventeenth-century English philosopher,
rejected the occupation theory, which held that all property was owned by society until social contracts allowed

individuals to secure property by occupation. Instead, Locke articulated the idea, based on natural law, that ownership of property originates through the exertion of labor on natural resources. Labor legitimizes ownership.[16] This shift in thinking about what legitimizes ownership is important and still relevant today. Does society grant ownership to individuals, or does individual labor legitimize ownership? This question is related to a century-old debate over whether individual freedom takes precedence over societal well-being or the goal of societal well-being justifies restrictions on individual freedom. And it also points toward the foundation of our economic model—namely to the role of entrepreneurship, which is rewarded by the results of the labor of individuals.

"Impact businesses" and Just Banking institutions aim to bridge this polarity between individual freedom and societal well-being. Just Banking principles require asking how private ownership relates to the public good. What are the rights and responsibilities of ownership, and how can ownership models be designed in such a way as to bridge the tension between private ownership and the well-being of society? Ownership becomes more than a private affair even as it creates the basis for personal accountability and entrepreneurship.

Because deciding on a governance structure is so important, the next section identifies a set of questions and criteria that can guide this process of assessing the advantages and disadvantages of particular governance models for mission-driven businesses.

Governance Models: Asking the Critical Questions

There is no one ideal governance model for all mission-driven businesses. Different regions of the world have different legal restrictions and possibilities; however, the following questions can be helpful in choosing a model.

1. Who is responsible? Making governance accountable. Defining accountability and responsibility is the primary purpose of a governance structure. Holding leaders accountable for achieving the mission-based goals is a key part of this first anchor. Triodos Bank did this by creating a legal construct in which a foundation oversees the mission and voting rights while also allowing individual investors to benefit financially.

2. Who brings the skills and capabilities? Making governance competent. Running a business requires skill, knowledge, and capacity. Successful banks design their governance structures to incorporate people with these attributes. A cooperative bank might struggle to identify board members with the skill set needed to oversee the governance of a financial institution; the NGO or foundation that governs a bank might have the right values alignment but lack business acumen. Finding ways to ensure that the right professional skills and the mission focus are balanced in the governance structure is one of the core challenges of mission-based businesses.

3. Who is affected? Connecting governance with impact. The third guiding question for developing a governance structure that anchors the mission is about creating the connection between decision-makers and those affected by the business. Depending on the purpose of the organization, those who are affected could be the community, the employees, or the environment; some banks also consider the interests of future generations and create a "voice" for them in their decision-making process. Bringing all of these voices into the governance body can create space for meaningful dialogue about how to align decisions with the goals of the mission.

Organizational Structure

The governance structure is the first anchor of the mission, but it is not sufficient to ensure that financial institutions balance impact and profitability in the long run. Operating with a mission requires Just Banking institutions to (1) embed impact objectives throughout the organization and (2) develop tools and methods for impact assessment that make visible whether and how the impact objectives are being reached. Both steps may require adding qualitative benchmarks to the operation. These impact goals are often harder to quantify than profit and efficiency objectives.

The Case of Banca Popolare Etica: Inviting Members into the Organization

Banca Popolare Etica, a cooperative bank in Italy, responded to the need to anchor impact in their lending decisions by including its member-owners in the impact assessment process of evaluating loan applications. Cesare Vitali, the head of research at Banca Popolare Etica, described this process:

> We have a process in addition to the economic evaluation called a Social and Environmental Evaluation that we do for business loans. ... It's one of the most powerful ways to understand if our clients ... are compliant with our values and with our way of banking. It's also really important to evaluate our clients from a social and environmental point of view, in order to strengthen the CSR [corporate social responsibility] profile of our client. For the last few years, we are seeing more clients thanking us for the evaluation because they began to integrate more values into their business.[17]

At Banca Popolare Etica the evaluations are divided into three main steps: (1) the social environmental questionnaire, (2) the credit analysis, and (3) the social environmental evaluation by member volunteers of the bank called "social evaluators." Says Vitali:

> The most important step is that social evaluators go to meet and interview our clients ... about how the client has responded to the set of indicators and the questions we asked earlier in the evaluation. They are also trained by us, the bank. ... So they really help us a lot in giving our evaluations a more integrated and a more complete profile. At the end of the process, we have an integrated evaluation of our client and in order to give the loan, both evaluations should be positive.[18]

Banca Popolare Etica does two things: (1) It uses the impact evaluation as a tool to decide on a loan application and to provide a service to the loan client. The evaluation helps the client better understand its social and environment impact. (2) By including its members in the evaluation process, the bank creates a meaningful dialogue with members about decisions the bank makes. Having members evaluate loans is also a way of making the bank accountable to its stakeholders. In this case, the loan does not go forward without the approval of the social evaluator.

This loan evaluation process by members of a cooperative bank is an example of how anchoring the mission in the organizational structure leads to innovations in operation and processes. While these policies and structures help anchor the mission and keep it alive in the bank, the level of transparency required also poses a risk for the bank by creating opportunities for criticism and scrutiny of the bank's operation.

Building a Mission-Based Organization

In our work with mission-based financial institutions, we seek to explore and understand best practices in anchoring a mission in an organization. There is no one-size-fits-all formula for developing structures, practices, and policies because geography, culture, the regulatory environment, and other factors all play a role in which solutions will be relevant and which will not. That said, we have found the organizational iceberg (developed by Edgar Schein at MIT) to be an effective conceptual tool for exploring this question (see figure 2.2).[19]

It is widely observed that the tip of an iceberg is visible to everyone, while the larger part of the iceberg is hidden

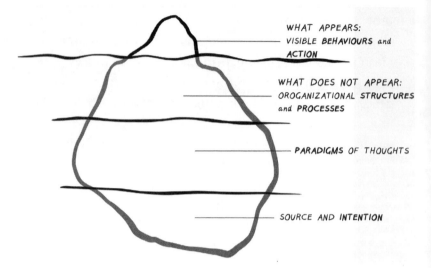

WHAT APPEARS:
VISIBLE BEHAVIOURS and
ACTION

WHAT DOES NOT APPEAR:
OROGANIZATIONAL STRUCTURES
and PROCESSES

PARADIGMS OF THOUGHTS

SOURCE AND INTENTION

Figure 2.2
Iceberg model of organizational reality

beneath the water. The iceberg model portrays an organization's operations in the same way: some of its processes are more visible than others. For example, the financial products a bank offers, its branding and communications, and its network of branches are all visible manifestations of the organization. They reflect its corporate identity and create a tangible interface with the organizational culture. Less visible but no less important are the structures and processes that define the operation and determine the success or failure of the business. When challenges arise, organizations often respond by adjusting their structures and processes to the new demands.

But as anyone who has been involved in a change process understands, there is an even less visible organizational layer that is still highly relevant. Schein calls this the "mental model" or thought paradigm.[20] Our mental model—the way we think—affects how we work. For example, do I fundamentally believe that a business can be mission-driven rather than profit-driven? The answer to that question will shape my actions and decisions. Mission-based banks need to understand how the mission translates across all levels of the organization—from financial products to the core structures and practices to the intention that everyone in the organization (especially the leaders) brings to their work. The alignment of the mission across these organizational levels is a critical anchor that enables balancing mission and profit. It often requires internal innovation around structures, policies, and practices.

For years we ran a community of practice with HR managers from mission-based banks around the world. This work produced many valuable insights and highlighted for us the extent to which standard business practices must be adapted to anchor the mission. For example, a question the HR managers that we work with discuss regularly is whether every employee in a mission-based financial institution must personally subscribe to the mission.

In a coworker meeting at Triodos Bank in the Netherlands, we joined an interesting discussion that illustrates this point. One managing director thought it should be mandatory for all coworkers to have an account with Triodos Bank. The CEO, to our surprise, disagreed. He wanted the coworkers to have the option to say yes or no to banking with Triodos. As freedom and self-determination are important values for the organization, taking the option to say no away from coworkers would be contradictory. Authentically anchoring the value of freedom and self-determination in the organization means taking the risk that coworkers would choose to bank with someone else. Anchoring the impact objectives affects all levels of the organizational reality—the actions, behaviors, structure, and processes, but also the thinking and the intention that everyone brings to work every day.

In Vancouver, Vancity Credit Union's approach is to create opportunities for all employees to develop a deeper understanding of the mission and the work of the credit union and to opt in to that mission and its implications through a weeklong "Orientation Immersion" program.

Vancity's HR and learning department created the program because the organization recognized it is difficult to understand what working in a Just Banking institution means until you experience it. The orientation is designed to help new hires "feel the difference" and understand the credit union's work, though all employees are encouraged to complete the program. The five-day program includes classroom-like experiences and visits to business members of the credit union, as well as time for creative problem solving, dialogue, and reflection. Says Colin Cuthbert, a learning consultant at Vancity:

> One of the important moments of the program comes on the last day, when the theme is "Vancity and You." This is when the facilitators introduce a "point of choice." They say to participants, "If, after this week's experiences, Vancity doesn't look like a good fit for you, now is the time to walk away." In fact, the credit union offers to compensate participants with a week's wages if they do decide to walk away.

This crucial moment is Vancity's way of demonstrating how serious it is about its values and mission. A lot of organizations claim to be values-based, and they share a list of "official" values. But Vancity wants to make sure that participants understand that this organization is different. Vancity takes its commitment to values so seriously that it wants employees to reflect about whether their values align with the organization's, and then decide whether to stay or not. Only three people have ever taken the option to walk away since its launch, but Vancity still finds this point of choice is a key element of what one might call a "conscious onboarding" process. I have found, as both an alum of the program and now as a facilitator, that Vancity's Orientation Immersion week leaves people excited and energized. For employees both old and new, Orientation Immersion offers an opportunity for connection to and deep understanding of Vancity's vision and culture. It also creates valuable networking opportunities for participants, who get to meet people from all levels and departments throughout the organization. This cross-pollination creates a stronger sense of community, while also giving entry-level hires an idea of the career pathways that can be open to them.[21]

Quantitative objectives have a tendency to dominate because they can be easily calculated and communicated. Impact is harder and more complex to measure, communicate, and evaluate. Vancity developed its orientation program as a way of embedding the mission-driven culture across the organization in order to affect behavior and decision-making at all levels. Anchoring the mission in this way takes substantial effort, and the onboarding process at Vancity recognizes this.

Another common theme among the HR directors is hiring for mission skills or business skills. Just Banking businesses don't always find it easy to identify people who possess both the impact focus and the appropriate professional skill set. In one session with HR professionals we heard the following: "At first, we hired for values and searched for candidates that bring experience regarding the impact we want to have. But then we realized that the organization lacked professional skills. So we jumped back and hired for professional banking skills. But then we saw the impact going down. Balancing both sides and creating an organization where both skill sets are respected and thrive is the real challenge and the real innovation."[22]

Els Verhagen, Triodos Bank's HR director, described interview practices she developed in recognition of the fact that conventional practices don't always work in a business that combines impact with profit: "Values need to be lived. I have learned that the connection between the individual values of the coworker and the organizational values is very important. Only when you deeply understand your own values are you able to take values-based decisions and act with values. We need an ongoing dialogue about values, not a list that hangs on the wall." She went on to describe how she talks about values with a candidate in an interview: "When I conduct interviews, I take a close look at the decision points and changes in a biography and focus a part of my interview on these points. What made you take this decision? Why did you do this? From my experience, these are the moments when I learn most about the underlying values of an applicant."[23]

On the question of performance management, Andrea Parnell, head of HR at Southern Bancorp said: "One specific thing that we're working on with performance management this year is coming up with mission-based goals. Historically, we've had margin-based goals: growing deposits, growing loans, those kinds of things; but we're coming up with goals that are related to our mission and translating that down to every single job in the organization. That allows people to connect the dots between what they do every day and how it connects back to our bigger purpose."[24] Mission-based goals look, for example, at the impact of loans on the community. Parnell's approach to anchoring the mission recognizes the importance of creating tools that help coworkers engage with the mission by consistently translating "the bigger purpose" into the day-to-day.

GLS Bank in Germany has a compensation scheme that inverts the relationship between work and income: instead of "I work so that I receive income," its philosophy is "I receive income so that I can work." In this view, income enables an employee to spend his or her time and talent in the bank; income is not the reward. The underlying thinking is that, ideally, an engaged team member does not need incentives to work but wants to grow and develop while doing work that he or she is passionate about. GLS Bank bases its compensation scheme on this thinking:

- Everyone receives a base income, which constitutes the starting point of the payment scheme. This base income should enable coworkers to live well.

- Any additional compensation is based on two factors:
  1. whether the coworker has dependents or particularly high housing costs (as in expensive cities);[25] and

2. the functional group the coworker part of, as defined by GLS Bank. GLS Bank identifies eight functional groups that are based on level of education, the range of responsibility that a coworker holds, and the number of years of experience.

- There are no bonus payments.

Though this compensation scheme is highly contextual and would be illegal in the United States, it illustrates the types of radical shifts that can take place when incorporating mission goals into otherwise mundane structures. In the Just Banking institutions, we work with, we see this reworking of policy, practice, and structure in all aspects of the business, from risk management to procurement to expectations for client interactions, and more.

Which brings us to the deepest level of the iceberg model in figure 2.2: the intention. Intention is closely related to the third anchor of the mission: leadership.

Leadership

In our work with Just Banking institutions, we have created a leadership development program for high-potential leaders from mission-based banks around the globe.[26] An essential element of the program is when leaders work on their personal leadership intention: Why do I work in this bank? What do I want to bring into the organization? The intention a leader holds is crucial for the effectiveness of their work.

To better understand this level of the iceberg, we look at the research of Otto Scharmer, senior lecturer at MIT's Sloan School of Management. In a research interview with Bill O'Brien, the former CEO of Hanover Insurance, Scharmer asked what he had learned from years of leading and initiating change in his organization. O'Brien responded, "The success of an intervention depends on the interior condition of the intervener."[27] O'Brien argues that the intention we hold affects the outcome of our actions. The intention that I bring into a meeting, a change process, or a project has an impact on the success of the work. Our intention affects the quality and results of our actions.

We have all experienced this. Long-term behavioral change requires addressing how we think about a problem and what intention we hold. If we don't change our thinking, we won't change our behavior, and we will just repeat the patterns of the past. Leading with intention therefore constitutes a critical third anchor of a mission-oriented organization.

Scharmer has developed an innovation and leadership method called Theory U that enables leaders to break through old patterns and access deeper levels of intention. Scharmer poses two core questions to leaders: Who is my Self? And what is my Work? [28] Self with a capital S refers to one's highest future potential as a person. Work with a capital W refers to the deeper purpose of the work.

When we work with leaders in Just Banking businesses, we invite them to explore these questions. Answering them requires a personal practice of self-reflection. It also requires a community of learning. Exploring the questions cannot be done alone in an office. Finding answers requires a leader to engage in a dialogue that connects two experiences: one, the impact of his or her own work, especially from the perspective of those with no voice; and two, an internal dialogue, in which one turns the beam of observation back onto oneself. The self is the ultimate anchor of an intention, the only possible anchor. This anchoring allows leaders to lead their teams, the business, and themselves authentically, and also to step into unknown territory.

Dayna Cunningham, the executive director of MIT's Community Innovators Lab, or CoLab, describes the process of articulating this intention for a leader as finding your own North Star and using it to navigate unfamiliar terrain: "The North Star is the image for my own direction as a leader, the intention I hold. The North Star gives me direction when I am lost or in moments of disruptive change and challenges. It is something that guides me."[29]

Finding your own North Star as a leader in a mission-driven organization means anchoring your intention for yourself. Impact businesses innovate by stepping away from the mainstream model. Doing so requires a clear direction, with a North Star as an orientation point.

Today, unprecedented challenges threaten the planet, our democracies, and our well-being. The complexity of these problems requires us to step into unfamiliar territory and respond in new ways. Identifying one's own North Star or leadership intention is the foundation of the process.

Table 2.2
Three institutional anchors of Just Banking

	Anchor		
	Governance	Organization	Intentional Leadership
Objective	Legal structure reflects the objectives of both profit and mission	Reinvent practices across all levels of the business	Articulate and anchor the intention as a leadership practice

Three Institutional Anchors

Operating a mission-based bank that uses finance as a tool for social change requires anchoring this objective; otherwise the quantitative pull of the profit objective will dominate. Table 2.2 summarizes the core concepts for anchoring an intention.

Just Banking requires reinventing how a bank operates in order to integrate the expanded objectives into the daily operations. Without these three institutional anchors, the idea of Just Banking risks being watered down over time and becoming a public relations strategy not backed by real practice and impact.

These three anchors create the conditions for financial institutions to succeed in operating on Just Banking principles. Although interest in impact banking and investment has grown, this form of banking and finance is still a niche operation in the financial services world. The following chapter examines why this is so and identifies some of the systemic barriers to banking based on mission.

3
Systemic Challenges and Opportunities of Just Banking

Just Banking institutions are niche players in the financial system. While they innovate and experiment with new ideas and practices, their size and impact are marginal in comparison with those of other financial institutions. The largest actors in the financial sector shape the market and define the environment in which all financial institutions operate. Though Just Banking institutions are small, the practices emerging from these institutions offer lessons that can influence the whole sector.

Systemic Challenges of the Financial Sector

The financial sector today is dominated by a concentration of large players in the market, some large enough to be called "systemically important financial institutions" (SIFIs), meaning the collapse of even one of them could pose a risk to the overall economy. To use the familiar jargon, they are "too big to fail." A second important characteristic of the financial sector is that it has grown disproportionally in comparison with the rest of the economy over the past thirty years, which has led to what is called the "financialization" of the economy.[1] In 2019 in the United States the financial sector reached about 21 percent of GDP; in 1947, it was 10 percent.[2] This trend is also reflected in a disproportional increase in profits in the financial sector and in soaring executive pay. While the size of the financial sector allows for economies of scale, and large businesses in nonfinancial industries need financial partners of a similar size, size can pose risks to the overall economy. These risks have been offloaded to taxpayers and are not borne by the banks themselves, as failure of these large financial institutions could lead to economic collapse. In addition, a revolving door between the financial sector and its regulators leads to a lack of oversight and less effective regulation of the sector.[3] Finally, the increasing volume of highly speculative financial products with low or no value in the nonfinancial or real economy leads to questions about the purpose of finance and the possible negative impact of financial speculation on the rest of the economy, especially in the form of a real estate bubble.[4]

The taxpayer bailout of failing banks during the financial crisis of the early 2000s led to a strong public reaction to the existing structure of the financial sector and to questions about the purpose and impact of financial institutions. While the purpose of finance is to facilitate monetary transactions and thereby provide stability to the overall economy, the current concentrated structure, with a high volume of speculative financial products, does not provide the stability that the economy needs, nor does the sector effectively provide loans and investments in areas of the economy where they are most needed.

As questions about the role and responsibility of the financial sector grow louder, the demand for alternatives is rising. More and more customers are looking for financial institutions aligned with their interests and values that provide products with a positive impact on society. They are looking for financial players focused on the well-being of the real economy and of society as a whole, a quest that creates new opportunities for innovations in the field of Just Banking. This chapter discusses the systemic challenges within the current financial system, as well as the opportunities for Just Banks operating in this environment.

Systemic Challenges for Just Banking Institutions

Just Banking institutions are affected by how the wider financial sector operates. The size of large players in the sector, the high yields some banks earn, and rapid technological advances create an environment that makes it difficult for niche players like Just Banking institutions to compete and be successful. What follows is a brief look at some of the core challenges and limitations Just Banking institutions face.

Competition for Capital and Talent

Just Banking institutions compete with mainstream banks for capital and talent. All banks need depositors or investors. Conventional economic theory argues that capital allocation should follow profitability, and we know the high returns that speculative financial products can earn are rarely possible with banking products based on real economy transactions, especially in the short run. Many argue that if small banks cannot compete on investor returns, they will not be able to attract capital.[5]

The very existence of Just Banking institutions challenges this narrative. They are profitable businesses attracting clients and investors. How do they compete for capital? Insofar as people today face profoundly disruptive externalities, such as the climate crisis or inequality and marginalization of communities, more and more investors see the conventional approach falling short and seek out investments that consider externalities. It is still a challenge for Just Banking institutions to compete with mainstream institutions, but the field is shifting.

The same argument applies to the ability of a bank to attract talent. Though talent is more local than financial capital, most Just Banking institutions cannot pay salaries that compete with what mainstream financial institutions can offer. Just Banking institutions must rely on highly qualified individuals taking the purpose of their work and the impact they create into account when making career decisions.

Contextual Awareness versus Standardization

Just Banking institutions are what we call "context-aware." As a community bank, City First Bank in Washington, D.C., needs to understand and closely interact with its community partners to provide the services and products that create a positive impact; to reach its environmental impact objectives, including countering the climate crisis, GLS Bank in Germany needs to understand the pros and cons of different renewable energy solutions and the root causes of climate change; and BRAC Bank staff in Bangladesh must invest a disproportional amount of time to serve the bank's SME clients effectively who sometimes have only limited reading skills or no standard accounting practices.

If these high-context financial products operate at one end of a spectrum, speculative financial products that have only the remotest connection to the real economy are at the other end. Just Banking institutions lend and invest with a level of complexity and plurality that runs counter to the efficiency and standardization the mainstream financial sector strives for. The conflict between the high speed of finance and the lower speed of analyzing and understanding context and impact constitutes a structural challenge for the relationship between finance and the real economy that affects not only Just Banking but the industry as a whole. Just Banking institutions have made these structural issues more visible in their attempt to bridge the gap between context and standardization.

Regulation

In the aftermath of the global financial crisis, the regulatory environment of the financial sector changed. New regulations increased consumer protection and instituted higher capital requirements for banks.[6] These regulations were written primarily with larger financial players in mind. The burden on small and medium-sized financial institutions, many of which struggle to respond to new regulatory demands, often goes unnoticed.

But critics argue that these new regulations did not go far enough in addressing the root causes of the crisis or limiting the systemic risks within the sector. Examples of regulations that would address these systemic risks include reinstating the separation of commercial (depository) and investment banking established by the Glass-Steagall Act of 1933 and breaking up institutions that are "too big to fail."

Just Banking institutions struggle with three core challenges in this new regulatory environment. First, most regulation is designed for large businesses with trained staff whose full-time job is working with regulators. Small and medium-sized banks do not have the same resources and, as a result, struggle with a higher workload and higher costs. Small banks find it challenging to handle processes and reporting structures that regulators demand, and that sometimes seem irrelevant to a small or medium-sized bank with a focus on the real economy. Second, from the perspective of the regulator, it is easier to devise regulations for large businesses with departments specialized on regulations than for a diverse set of smaller banks that operate locally and offer more individualized products and services. Regulation discourages context awareness by demanding standardization of bank operations. Third, the concept of Just Banking often is unfamiliar to regulators. Says one executive of a Just Banking institution: "Our highest risk is that customers don't trust us anymore to create the impact we claim. So, that is the real risk." Regulators who are not familiar with Just Banking practices may also struggle to understand the decisions underlying a Just Bank's lending portfolio.

Speed of Technological Change

Although new technologies, such as blockchain, are hyped as tools of democratization of finance and may be perfect for decentralized innovations in the financial sector, in reality, large financial players dominate the field of digitization and technological innovation in finance. Smaller banks and Just Banking institutions often lack the resources or partners to use new technologies to their advantage. We see exceptions to this rule, but by and large, Just Banking institutions are not first -movers in this sector. As a result, most new technologies are not designed with Just Banking principles in mind.

Mental Models about the Purpose and Role of Banking

The final challenge is less visible but nevertheless important. Mental models describe our assumptions about the world around us and conceptual frameworks that guide our thinking. Change theory teaches us that initiating and sustaining profound change requires us to address the mental models that underlie our actions.

Banks that operate according to Just Banking principles contradict the dominant mental model about the purpose and role of banking. In a paradigm that sees banks as profit maximizers, Just Banking institutions do not fit into the predominant existing framework of banking. The implications are both deep and tangible, ranging from regulators not recognizing the banking model, to educational systems not teaching this form of banking, to media not reporting on Just Banking institutions.

Opportunities: Milestones in the History of Financial Impact Innovations

Throughout the history of finance there have been innovations that use finance as a tool for positive change. Some of these innovations were reactions to the challenges created by the mainstream financial sector. Table 3.1 presents a snapshot of some of the milestones in the field of financial impact innovation.

Each of these innovations has developed its own practices and solutions using finance as a tool for positive impact. To better understand how these organizations and their innovations function, we take a closer look at examples in each category.

1.   Financial Institutions with Impact Objectives

Financial institutions that aim for a positive social or environmental impact have been the source of many financial innovations. Around the world we find different models of Just Banking operations, and the following pages look briefly at the history of two of them, credit unions and, as US-specific example, community development financial institutions.

Credit unions   Credit unions are cooperatively owned financial institutions governed by their members on the principle of one member, one vote. In practice, this structure

Table 3.1
Types of financial innovations aiming for positive social and environmental impact

Organization	Examples	Innovation	Limitation
Banks and financial institutions	• Credit unions • Community development financial institutions • Cooperative banks • Public banks	• Serve underbanked and unbanked customers • Balance profit with impact	• Challenged to balance impact with standardization • Lack of impact measurement tools
Investment approaches	• Funds dedicated to socially responsible investing • ESGs principles (environmental, social, and governance) investing • Triple bottom line in finance (people, planet, profit) • Impact investment	• Use finance to create positive societal impact • Blending of financial with social and environmental bottom line • Introduced a new paradigm of investment management	• Absence of common standards and metrics for measuring impact • Challenged to scale up

(continued)

Table 3.1 (continued)

Organization	Examples	Innovation	Limitation
Development finance	• Microfinance	• Financial services for the poor and unbanked • Focus on women • Lending products that do not require traditional collateral	• Actors in the market that misuse microfinance • Challenged to understand quality-of-life improvement
Fintechs for social impact	• Businesses providing selected financial services, e.g., for remittances (bKash)	• Highly scalable, consumer-friendly financial products • Highly accessible	• High up-front costs and ongoing investment needed • Lack of impact-focused investors

requires credit unions to reinvest all profits back into the business, the members, and the communities they serve. This ownership model helps anchor a mission of solidarity and impact in the business.

The idea of credit unions goes back to the 1840s in England; it arrived in the United States in 1908.[7] By 1930, 1,100 credit unions were operating in the United States. Their number grew to 23,000 by 1969, before beginning to decline in the 1970s. Today, only about 6,000 operate in the United States, but many more operate around the world. Although the number of credit unions in the United States has declined, their membership and assets are growing steadily. The roughly 6,000 credit unions in the United States today serve more than 117.3 million members—43.7 percent of the economically active population. They hold total assets of $1.51 trillion.[8]

Historically, credit unions have been formed around a specific bond of association, often created by unbanked or underbanked communities to pool limited resources and serve their members. Membership groups that have founded credit unions include teachers, farmers, firefighters, and immigrant associations, among many others. The membership restriction has loosened over time in the United States but still remains a strong part of the culture and character of credit unions. In the United States in the 1970s, the National Credit Union Administration (NCUA), which was created as an independent agency to regulate credit unions, supported credit unions' expansion of their product lines and desire to ease membership restrictions.[9] These new conditions allowed US credit unions to grow and expand their assets from $12.5 billion in 1971 to $64.5 billion ten years later. By 1991 the assets of credit unions topped $225 billion; by 2019 they had reached $1.4 trillion. At the same time, however, the number of mergers of credit unions increased and has been one reason for the continuing decline in the total number of credit unions in the United States.[10]

This history tells a success story, but it also points at tensions in the industry. Some in the financial industry believe that credit unions, because of their size, profitability, and loosened bonds of association, no longer deserve their nonprofit status. Since the 1970s, several lawsuits against the NCUA have been filed along these lines.[11] Credit unions counter this charge with the argument that all profits are returned to members. Regardless of the motivation behind the lawsuits, they raise important questions. How efficient and profitable can a credit union become before it begins to act like a mainstream financial institution? We see large credit unions that manage to walk this line and others that operate more like conventional banks.

The concept of the anchoring triangle that we presented in chapter 2 argues that anchoring a mission in an organization requires three anchors: governance, organization, and leadership. The ownership model helps anchor the founding idea of solidarity and self-help in credit unions, but this is not sufficient when the leadership and organizational structures of a credit union do not do the same.

Community development financial institutions Community development financial institutions (CDFIs) are a US-based model of financial institutions that aim for positive impact. CDFIs can take different forms, such as banks, credit unions, loan funds, microloan funds, or venture capital providers. The core innovation of CDFIs is that they provide financial services to underserved communities and bridge banking with access to development funds such as philanthropic or government support.

The origin of CDFIs is rooted in the "black banking" movement.[12] The civil rights movement launched numerous models for financial institutions serving black communities and with that built the pathway to CDFIs by proving that financial institutions that serve minority communities can create positive impact.[13] Running a small financial institution is challenging in itself, but when the community being served experiences direct and structural violence, the impact on the community and its infrastructure can be devastating.[14] At the end of the 1960s the black banking movement laid the foundation for CDFIs.

Chicago's South Shore Bank (later renamed Shore Bank) was founded in 1973 in a redlined community that faced deep disinvestment and racial discrimination. It was the first community investment bank and developed the model for community development banking.[15] Among its many accomplishments, the bank served as proof of concept for the 1977 Community Reinvestment Act (CRA), which encourages regulated financial institutions to invest in the communities that are located in.

Building on the framework established by the CRA, the federal CDFI Fund was created in 1994 and modeled after a similar fund created by private foundations in the 1960s. The

CDFI Fund is a federal program supporting certified CDFIs. Its purpose is to promote economic revitalization and community development in low-income communities through investment in and assistance to CDFIs. While the CDFI Fund faces several challenges, from political opposition to criticism of its administrative processes, it provides relevant support for entrepreneurship in low-income communities in the United States today.[16]

A key innovation of CDFIs is to use a financial institution to create a bridge for development funding between philanthropic or government investments and community entrepreneurs. The movement has also created influential if less visible innovations to serve communities with highly contextualized financial services. Brian Argrett, CEO of City First in Washington, D.C.,[17] describes what that entails:

> You really have to be engaged and not work from
> afar, ... throwing in benefits or throwing in opportunities. ...
> As a bank, you're not doing the work. You're providing the
> capital to those who are doing the work. So, what it means
> is, you have to be very intentional, who you're choosing to
> work with and who you're choosing to partner with to figure
> out what work needs to be done. Sounds easy, but it's not
> necessarily because everyone has different interests in an
> evolving community.
>
>   For example, ... we're having a large forum—we're
> calling it a community development finance conferences or
> forums. ... we're bringing together all of the stakeholders who
> might be involved and might be interested in a more equitable
> economic development east of the river. So this is a community
> in Washington where economic development is coming,
> and the question is, as it comes, how can we make sure that

resources are more fully shared by the community? To do that, you need to bring together everyone who has a stake, including the city government, the residents, and the nonprofits that are working within that community, the for-profit developers who will have an interest in the commercial corridors, and housing, and the nonprofit providers, as well as other financing sources.

What we're trying to do is bring them together, talk about the tough issues, everything from gentrification, to job creation, to entrepreneurialism within a specific community, and come out of that with hopefully stronger connections, better insight, maybe a … policy paper to [help us] decide how we should encourage this on a go-forward basis. Then, of course, for ourselves, greater clarity on where the needs are and how they might be bridged. So things like that, which you can't do every day, but when you have the opportunity to do, can give you great insight and also connects you in a greater manner to the other folks who are involved, engaged, and interested in whatever that charge might be. In this case, equitable development within this community.[18]

To finance change, City First Bank needs to identify the right partners to work with. But the process Brian Argrett describes goes beyond financing. The bank facilitates a dialogue between different stakeholders in the community. CDFIs understand that banks cannot bring about change on their own; rather, they finance, collaborate with, and facilitate those who are leading change.

2. Investing with Impact

Investment funds bundle investments from different investors and place them under professional management. Historically, the idea of designing investment funds with a social impact became popular with the socially responsible investing (SRI) movement in the late 1970s and early 1980s. Today, core concepts for investment funds with impact include (1) SRI, (2) the environmental, social, and governance (ESG), principles, (3) the triple-bottom-line concept (people, planet, profit), and (4) impact investment. Though these approaches differ in their details, all include the social or environmental impact on society in investment decisions and reflect an increasing demand to align investments with impact. The different names and descriptors reflect an underlying challenge in the field: how to set standards and common measurements, and a lack of regulation, which makes it difficult to distinguish positive impact from "greenwashing" or "impact washing"—when investments are made to seem more impactful than they are.[19] The criticism that there are no uniform standards for investing under these rubrics has been articulated for some time.[20] Depending on whom you talk to in this fast-growing field, the answers, processes, and practices differ. Let's compare some of the core concepts. Again, these are examples; the field itself is much broader.

Socially responsible investing   Socially responsible investing (SRI) has its origins in efforts to connect the work of grassroots social movements to the movement of money. The core tenet is that money has more than just cash value; it is a political tool that can be used—through divestment, investment, or shareholder advocacy—to work in solidarity with social movements to push for change. Likely the most famous example is the drive in the 1970s and 1980s to divest from companies based in South Africa in support of the anti-apartheid movement. Under pressure from investors, American companies and other institutions largely divested from South Africa. The strain this massive divestment placed on the South African economy eventually led a coalition of South African companies to draft a charter calling for the end of the racist system.

SRI introduced the idea of aligning finance with people's values and can be credited with developing practices for how to do so. SRI began to articulate, for example, exclusion criteria to ensure that investments would not contradict the values of the investor. In retrospect, SRI has played a fundamental role in bridging a movement on the street calling for social change with mainstream finance. By creating this connection, SRI pushed thinking about the role of finance into new territory. It is the foundation of impact investing today.

Triple-bottom-line framework: People, planet, and profit   The SRI movement that launched in the 1980s was followed by the success of a concept called triple-bottom-line (TBL), a term coined by John Elkington at the end of the 1990s.[21] SRI had introduced and prototyped the idea of aligning an investment decision with the values of the investors. But to actually align them requires understanding the impact of a business. The TBL concept answers this by expanding reporting from a single bottom line (profit) to two other bottom lines: the impact on people (social bottom line) and the impact on the planet (environmental bottom line).

Though the TBL concept enjoys wide popularity and has influenced thinking about sustainable business practices in organizations across the world, in 2018 Elkington issued a "recall" of the TBL concept. His original intention for TBL, to help people rethink capitalism and the economy as a whole, had not been achieved, he thought. Instead, he felt that the TBL concept had been reduced to just another accounting system, another business framework. "None of these sustainability frameworks will be enough, as long as they lack the suitable pace and scale—the necessary radical intent—needed to stop us all overshooting our planetary boundaries," he has written.[22]

Elkington argues for a system perspective. What is needed is to fundamentally rethink how the economy as a whole operates, and not look just at individual investments or business decisions. Only from a system perspective is it possible to ascertain whether the economy as a whole has the impact we are aiming for. This form of system thinking is reflected in several concepts that followed the TBL framework and are known under such rubrics as the circular economy, the sharing economy, true cost accounting, and biomimicry, to name a few. All these models introduce a new economic paradigm. The concept of the circular economy, for example, suggests that economic decisions be modeled on how nature recycles all of its resources. The implication is that our economy can eliminate waste through a continual recycling of its resources, as opposed to the use-and-dispose character of a linear economy.

ESG principles In 2004 the United Nations secretary-general convened an international group of institutional investors to discuss how to connect social, environmental, and governance principles with investment decisions. This group formed the Principles for Responsible Investment (PRI) initiative, which today has over 2,500 signatories worldwide. The initiative was supported by a 2005 report, *Who Cares Wins*, which made the business case that integrating sustainability objectives into capital markets is good for business and good for society.[23] This initiative coined the term ESGs (environmental, social, and governance principles). The signatories of the UN initiative identified six principles to guide an ESG investment strategy.

> Principle 1: We will incorporate ESG issues into investment analysis and decision-making processes.
>
> Principle 2: We will be active owners and incorporate ESG issues into our ownership policies and practices.
>
> Principle 3: We will seek appropriate disclosure on ESG issues by the entities in which we invest.
>
> Principle 4: We will promote acceptance and implementation of the Principles within the investment industry.
>
> Principle 5: We will work together to enhance our effectiveness in implementing the Principles.
>
> Principle 6: We will each report on our activities and progress towards implementing the Principles.[24]

The ESG principles acknowledge environmental, social, and governance risks in operating businesses and that with these risks comes a fiduciary duty. The ESG principles do not exclude investments or promote specific focus areas such as green energy or living wages. A prominent example of an environmental risk for businesses is the impact of climate change on the insurance industry. Climate change causes more extreme weather patterns—with storms, floods, and wildfires resulting in increased insurance claims—and poses the question of what fiduciary duty insurance companies have when they recognize these risks.

The ESG principles are less a clear definition and guideline for investing than a political process for engaging businesses and encouraging them to take more responsibility for the negative externalities of their operation in their own interest. The ESG principles are based on a business rationale that translates social and environmental risks such as climate change into the costs of day-to-day business operations. The contribution of the ESG principles is a political engagement process for businesses.

Impact investment The latest example of combining finance with impact is the impact investing movement. While SRI laid the foundation for this field, impact investing today brings into the mainstream the idea of creating positive impact through investment decisions. The impact investing field was launched from a different societal perspective, namely, that of the philanthropic sector. In 2007 the Rockefeller Foundation convened a discussion on new ways to create impact other than through grants and donations.[25] The foundation defines impact investing as follows: "Impact investments are defined as investments made into companies, organizations, and funds with the intention to generate social or environmental impact alongside a financial return."[26] It is important to note that the launch of impact investing occurred at a time when some activists had begun questioning the investment strategies of foundations, arguing that the foundations' investments conflicted with their goals and mission statements.[27] Since then, the impact investment field has expanded even as it has struggled to find effective ways of measuring and communicating impact.[28]

Despite the challenges associated with measuring, understanding, and communicating the impact of investment decisions, impact investing has entered the mainstream. It is hard to find a major financial institution today that does not offer some sort of impact investment option. While the total volume of impact investments is difficult to quantify, and the tools for understanding and measuring impact are imperfect, impact investing has managed to change the industry.

This brief look at the field reveals a diversity of concepts, practices, and approaches, which are summarized in table 3.2. The storyline of innovations in the field of impact finance has moved from the margins to the mainstream in banking.

Each concept has a different set of practices that has contributed to Just Banking. An important shortcoming of all these different approaches, however, is the lack of uniform definitions, consistent terminology, and impact measurement standards. While there are several well-documented and researched proposals for measuring impact, including approaches that have been tested and applied, it is still difficult for investors to agree on how best to measure impact and to show how an investment aligns with their values.

3. Development Finance

Development finance aims for positive social impact by investing in regions with high economic or political risk.[29] Development finance employs some Just Banking practices. Though it is not possible to fully explore this complex topic here, we will look at microfinance as one prominent example.

Table 3.2
Innovations in the field of investment decisions

Investment concept	Founding idea	Innovation	Practices	Contribution to the field
SRI: socially responsible investing	Fight for human dignity, universal economic justice	• Connect investment decisions to values • Use investments to change corporate practices	• Transparency on social impact	• Introduced the idea of investing for social impact • Created a bridge between a movement on the street and investment decisions
Triple bottom line (people, planet, profit)	Changes in how businesses operate	• Use reporting practices to create transparency • Develop a new economic model	• Reporting standards for social and environmental impact	• Fostered a switch from individual investment decisions to aiming for system change

ESG: environmental, social, and governance principles	Business invited by UN secretary-general to commit to sustainable business practices as part of a new business strategy	Create a membership group that publicly commits to sustainable business practices	Reduction in corporate risks through sustainable practices	Made the business case for sustainable business practices
Impact investment	Launched by the philanthropic sector to increase capital investments in social and environmental causes	Enlist donors and investors in the fight for positive social change by creating investing opportunities aligned with impact objectives	Make impact investing options easily accessible to investors	Made the concept of impact investing mainstream

Microfinance Microfinance institutions provide financial services such as lending, making saving products available, and offering insurance for individuals and small businesses with no or limited access to mainstream banking. The lack of access to banking services often is due to poverty, social or geographic exclusion. After years of being valorized as the solution to ending poverty, microfinance fell off its pedestal around 2008. Research began to emerge that questioned the claim that microfinance ends or reduces poverty,[30] and damning reports were published describing the negative impacts of some microfinance products on clients. The microfinance industry went through a period of crisis, and it quickly became clear that the players in the field differ widely, as they do in any other part of the financial industry. What we know now is that assessing the impact of microfinance requires a deep analysis of the different actors.

Early forms of microfinance began to emerge in the mid-1970s, especially in Bangladesh, with BRAC Bank and the Grameen Bank. Shameran Abed, director of the Microfinance and Ultra Poor Programs at BRAC said the following in an interview:

> Our microfinance program really started to get off the ground in earnest in the late 1970s. We grew very quickly in the '80s and '90s, but still doing mostly traditional microfinance, which was the group-based loans mostly given out to women—very small ticket sizes. Over time our portfolio grew, and now (2015) we are doing a lot more than that, many different types of products and services, but still with a real focus on the unbanked at the base of the pyramid. So initially, it was mostly credit-led, but with some savings components in it. It was very basic products, very

rigid, because that's the way it was able to scale. It was very simple, accessible, and that was good for scale. ...

Wherever possible, we add savings as a product, which is very positive for the sector ... and more recently, we're seeing new types of products for risk mitigation, insurance, and even the beginnings of micro-pensions, and that's very good for the clients.

I think one of the advantages that our microfinance has is being very close to our clients. ... We used to have weekly collections. So, some member of our staff would meet every single one of our clients on a weekly basis. That kind of KYC (know your customers), which is not formal KYC, but an informal knowledge of your clients, what's happening in their lives, what's happening with their livelihoods. It's very powerful ... if organizations do what they can to ... gather all that information and data and see how that can be used to improve product offering, to improve service quality.[31]

BRAC is one of the most successful microfinance institutions in the world; it also provides services that go well beyond microfinance, such as health and education services, and develops programs for the ultra-poor who cannot be reached by microfinance. Shaman Abed describes BRAC's approach as having a close connection to the context and lives of the clients at the center of their work.

Today it is clear that microfinance institutions around the globe can have a life-changing impact on their clients, lifting them out of poverty, but in extreme cases microfinance institutions can destroy the lives of their clients—for example, by creating a debt spiral when loans cannot repaid because of high interest rates or by failing to support clients in ways that allow them to address the root causes of the challenges they face.[32] Juan Pablo Meza, CEO of SAC Apoyo Integral, a microfinance institution in El Salvador, explains: "How does the quality of life change when our customers receive a microfinance loan? We use a holistic approach to measure the impact of our loans, not focus[ing] only on the repayment rates."[33] Meza points out that microfinance lenders can be distinguished by the intention that underlies the operation. There are processes and structures that can ensure that microfinance benefits its clients, but all these structures can be corrupted or standardized in ways that don't serve the clients' well-being. For example, microfinance institutions that do not include quality-of-life indicators in their assessment process might miss a negative impact on the loan recipients. One possible negative impact of loans that are not designed to serve their recipients is overindebtedness, which can lead to a downward spiral for clients. Successful microfinance programs consider the environment the clients live in, the community, and the broader socioeconomic context. Only if the intention of a microfinance product is to improve clients' quality of life will it improve lives. Microfinance is an example of how the intention behind a financial product makes all the difference to the impact of this product.

4.   Fintech for Social Impact

Digital technologies in finance have changed the sector over the past decade and launched a new set of financial institutions, the so-called fintechs. The fintech sector builds new technological solutions, usually around a banking service, such as payments, remittances, or investments. Early fintech focused on the use of mobile phones for banking services; more recently, blockchain technologies have allowed the launch of cryptocurrencies, a form of secure, decentralized digital currencies. Though the sector is too young for a historical review, fintech represents a milestone in financial history that has affected the current status of Just Banking and will be relevant for the future.

While much of the field is profit-driven, there are examples of fintech institutions that use the opportunities created by digitization for impact innovations. These include Worldcoo, M-Pesa, Omisego, and Quipu Market.[34] Quipu Market, for example, is creating a community currency that allows informal economies with no or limited access to money to engage in economic activities.

Even when an institution or a technology application is intended to create a positive social impact, the devil is in the details. Blockchain, for example, provides a revolutionary opportunity to decentralize financial transactions but creates a large CO_2 footprint through the "mining" process—the addition of transactions to the ledger—and by design lacks an effective governance process. The search for technical solutions to complex social issues is fraught with failure and unintended consequences. Like Just Banking institutions, fintech institutions striving to achieve a positive societal impact need to make an intentional shift toward ecosystem awareness and address the same questions of how to anchor their mission through governance, organization, and leadership practices.

bKash—a Fintech with impact bKash developed an early mobile banking app that allows its users to receive money, make payments, recharge mobile balances, and pay bills. bKash was built to meet the needs of millions of rural, often poor Bangladeshis who depended on remittances from family members working outside the country or in different regions of the country. In April 2018 the World Bank Group estimated that about 266 million migrants and refugees worldwide sent or received remittances worth a total of US$689 billion.[35] Most of the beneficiaries of these payments are in low- and middle-income regions of the world. Remittances are often a financial lifeline for their recipients. Bangladesh received US$15.5 billion in remittances in 2018, accounting for 5.4 percent of GDP that year.

Sending money to family members in Bangladesh can be both costly and risky. In 2011, bKash was launched to address this challenge.[36] BRAC, the NGO, has a wide and highly distributed network across Bangladesh to serve poor Bangladeshis with health, educational, and microfinance services. bKash began to use this network when it launched in 2011, striving to serve poor and unbanked clients. Today bKash is one of the largest players in the field. Its infrastructure consists of a network of 80,000 agents in urban and rural areas, with over 30 million registered accounts in 2018. One key goal of bKash was to create accessibility for people at all income levels. Rather than relying on smart-phone technology, bKash can be accessed through even the cheapest mobile devices by entering an access code. It is accessible on 98 percent of the phones in Bangladesh. bKash is a subsidiary of

BRAC Bank and was founded in partnership with Money in Motion, the International Finance Corporation, and the Bill and Melinda Gates Foundation.

The story of bKash illustrates how an impact focus can lead to innovation in fintech banking. The driver for founding bKash was connected to BRAC's quest to serve poor Bangladeshis in rural areas. BRAC possessed the network and knowledge that allowed the innovation of bKash. Today bKash is a successful fintech business that also serves the banked and middle-income population of the country.

A Brief Journey through the History of Challenges and Opportunities in Just Banking

Just Banking institutions do not operate in isolation. They are embedded in a sector wrestling with systemic challenges. This brief journey has illustrated how innovations in Just Banking have emerged over time. Self-help initiatives launched financial institutions such as credit unions and CDFIs. When people's movements and investors' preferences aligned, a launching pad was created for the impact investing movement that is mainstream today. We are now poised on the edge of a new technological wave that seeks to integrate the learning and experiences in this field and create scalable solutions for the positive change that is desperately needed.

This chapter has identified some of the milestones that brought Just Banking institutions to where they are today. Just Banking institutions are innovations at the margin that are prototyping solutions for rethinking finance. Their practices are rooted in a long history of small innovations leading to successful blueprints that can be picked up, copied, and scaled up. But the challenge to understand, measure, and communicate impact remains. The next chapter focuses on this issue.

4
Learning Infrastructures for Understanding Impact

Just Banking is about impact. Understanding and measuring impact distinguishes Just Banking practices in the financial sector. While understanding the nonfinancial impact has been an issue for businesses around the globe for some time, practical ways of doing so are lagging behind. In 2019, a group of MIT researchers published an in-depth analysis comparing how rating agencies calculate indicators and rank businesses for their performance on environment, social, and governance dimensions.[1] The researchers found substantial discrepancies in the results, which they traced back to difficulties in selecting the right indicators, weighing different variables, and developing common standards for an industry. The MIT study exemplifies the challenge of measuring impact. Understanding impact from a social and environmental perspective requires moving beyond a single number to represent the success or failure of a business—namely, profit—and introducing a system that captures the qualitative impact of a business on the world.

We have seen inspiring examples of banks and financial institutions that have changed lives, transformed neighborhoods, and enabled social and green innovators and entrepreneurs to launch their businesses. Still, developing a strategy to create this impact reliably and understanding how to measure and capture it is a struggle for all the organizations we have worked with. We have found that the success of an impact strategy depends on how the organization manages to:

1. identify meaningful impact indicators and integrate an impact assessment process into the organization;

2. operate with a system perspective, meaning looking at impact from the perspective of the entire system while creating the impact measurement tools; and

3. build a continuous learning infrastructure to accompany the impact assessment.

Impact assessment tools need to match the strategic objectives of the organization, align with the organization's size and culture, and respond to the specifics of the sector in which the organization operates. Most important, the bankers we work with tell us that connecting the right measuring tool with a learning process is crucial.

Measuring Impact as a Learning Process in a Complex System

No one measurement system fits all exigencies. A tool that is useful for measuring impact today can become less useful over time. A tool that was successfully developed and implemented by the first user group may not have the same connection to the bank's intention with the second or third user group. Indicators can easily become numbers that lose their meaning. We have seen teams develop an impact dashboard, but the data collected were less meaningful for those who were not involved in the development work, and the dashboard was used by only a handful of team members. An impact assessment tool can even begin creating its own reality. Here is an example: in one conversation, a manager told us he introduced "number of jobs created" as a measure of impact. Two years later, he began to realize that his loan officers were missing out on opportunities because they looked at loan applications mainly through the lens of job creation, not as a way to help the neighborhood or launch a new business. The focus on the overall community impact had gotten lost. A measurement system that creates its own feedback loop will influence the behavior of those who use it.

Impact is an ever-moving target. One day a renewable energy technology may seem to help fight climate change, but a few years down the road, when we better understand its side effects, we may conclude that its negative impact outweighs the technology's benefits. We see the same thing in our daily lives. We switch to an electric car, but then realize we need to think about how the electricity we use to charge the car is generated and how to assess the environmental impact of its batteries. We become vegans to save CO_2 and then come to understand that the production of almond milk might have a larger negative water balance than we knew. Impact assessment requires taking the complexity of a system into account rather than isolating one variable. Understanding impact requires stepping back, looking at the big picture, and mapping the connections in a system. Change in one corner of a system will in turn create change in other parts of the system.

But this process of trial and error, of learning and reflection, is the key to measuring and understanding impact. Just Banking requires stepping into the context in order to understand the details of the reality in which banks operate, and then looking at the overall system. The process of wrestling with a dilemma, or taking a wrong step that leads to the right step, is what assessing impact is all about. Impact measurement without learning, dialogue, and reflection only leads to rankings that are meaningless or, in the worst case, counterproductive. Any metric can be used in ways that contradict its original purpose. The intention and the learning infrastructure that accompany the process of measuring impact are as central to the success of the evaluation as the numbers themselves.

The following two steps can help an organization design an effective impact measurement tool:

1. Create a learning infrastructure, an effective process for learning and engagement, to accompany the measurement process.

2. Use a system perspective to evaluate impact on the overall system, whether it is the organization, the sector, the community, or nature.

Figure 4.1 outlines four impact measurement approaches based on developing a learning infrastructure and a system

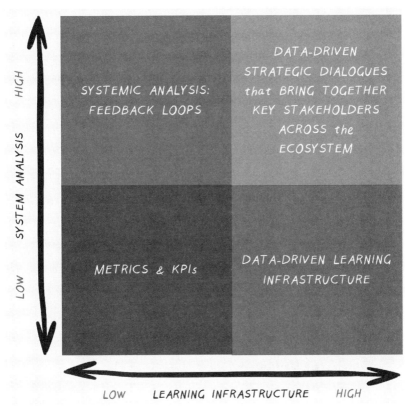

Figure 4.1
System transformation that incorporates a learning infrastructure

perspective. The approaches can be combined to inform each other.

Figure 4.1 describes options for integrating a system perspective with a learning infrastructure in an impact measurement process. Traditional impact indicators identify variables that measure itemized impact. Moving along the horizontal axis to the right quadrant suggests combining indicators with a learning infrastructure. Examples of learning infrastructures are dialogic spaces that include those involved in developing or using impact indicators to make sense of the data.

Moving along the vertical axis requires the generation of indicators from a system perspective. Systems are interconnected and define the context in which the indicators are embedded.[2] Developing indicators from a system perspective requires defining and identifying the system and understanding the feedback loops in the system. Finally, the upper right quadrant combines both axes to yield a learning infrastructure with a system perspective. Data are generated and stakeholders representing the whole ecosystem are included in the learning process based on the data analysis.

The next section explores learning infrastructures and the system perspective in more detail, as we consider them essential components of an effective impact measurement system.

Developing a Learning Infrastructure for Understanding Impact

An impact report is generated and sits on the desk of the managing director. Instead of stashing the report on a shelf, the director invites the relevant team members to discuss the data in the report and to launch a reflection and learning process. For example, B Corporations (B Corps, for short) are certified social and green businesses that use the data from their certification process to create customized feedback for their members. The data become a starting point for a learning process that includes a dialogue about impact. GLS Bank in Germany initiates conversations with its business clients based on its assessment of the possibilities for improving the businesses' impact.

A learning infrastructure can be created on any level of an organization, across organizational boundaries, or even at the level of society. Teams meet, leadership groups go on retreats, businesses create reports for customers and invite feedback. The options for using impact data to create learning processes are diverse, but the quality of these learning infrastructures needs to be high for their implementation to be meaningful. Just inviting folks to sit around a table and talk is not enough. What distinguishes learning infrastructures that are successful from those that fail is whether the process of evaluating impact data engages the participants in an open dialogue that is built on listening and reflection. Otherwise the result is a downloading exercise, after which participants leave the meeting with the same assumptions they brought to the meeting in the first place.

In working with teams, we sometimes suggest a simple tool for assessing the quality of a learning infrastructure: If you have not heard anything new, you have not listened. The quality of listening in a room defines the success of the learning process.

A second factor crucial to evaluating impact data is the adoption of a system perspective. Looking at the impact data from a system perspective introduces what learning theory calls double-loop learning. Double-loop learning occurs when a second loop is added to the learning process that requires the learner to look at the learning process itself.[3] An example will illustrate what we mean.

One focus area for Germany's GLS Bank is financing renewable energy. In launching a new impact assessment process, the bank asked whether its investments in renewable energy, although growing and successful, were capable of shifting the overall energy sector in Germany toward renewable energy. It didn't know the answer. So the bank articulated a vision for the future of renewable energy in Germany and outlined the steps and changes necessary to get there. GLS Bank then had to evaluate whether its investments were in line with this larger vision for renewable energy. The bank had been using a single-loop process of measuring the number of loans it made in renewable energy. Articulating a vision for impact transformation and aligning a loan program accordingly is a double-loop learning process that both assesses the loans and evaluates the impact those loans have on the system as a whole.

A double-loop learning infrastructure developed with a system perspective measures the data and then engages participants in a dialogue on system impact, systemic barriers to change, and interdependencies in the system. A system can be a sector such as renewable energy, a client group, or society at large.

A system perspective often requires more than analytical tools. If the voices in the room do not represent the whole system, relevant perspectives that are needed to find leverage points for transformation will be missing. Bringing these voices into the room is important. At the MIT Community Innovators Lab (CoLab), we describe this process as "innovation from the margins." Voices from the edges of a system often have a better understanding of where the system fails than voices at the center of the system. This idea has long been accepted in innovation concepts such as user-centric design, which requires innovators to put themselves in the position of extreme users and users at the edge of the system to identify openings for innovation.[4]

Why Bring Stakeholders into a Learning Infrastructure?

Businesses that want to understand impact from a system perspective benefit from inviting stakeholders into the room. Shameran Abed of the BRAC NGO in Bangladesh describes how BRAC moved beyond microfinance to design a program for the ultra-poor:

> If you look at the microfinance movement of the '80s and '90s, most of us as MFIs [microfinance institutions] used to say that microfinance basically serves the poorest. It took an organization like BRAC a long time to figure out that the very poorest, the people who are the most destitute, are not being reached by microfinance for a number of reasons. Microfinance institutions weren't able to get to these people because they were almost invisible within their own communities. Even the communities didn't see these people as full members because they were just too poor and too destitute. When we found this out, we realized that we needed to do more than traditional microfinance to be able to lift these people out of extreme, dire poverty. So we developed a different model and a different program, which we started in 2002 ... and now we've scaled up quite significantly in Bangladesh, and it has been piloted, and is now scaling in many other parts of the world. It's a two-year program, which is not just a financial services program, but it also tries to combine essential elements from social protection, financial services, and livelihoods. So, it's an

asset transfer grant-based program. It's a very intensive two-year program. It's a complex program to run, but if it's done well, we find that the results are tremendous. Over a two-year period, if the targeting is done well, if the interventions are provided well, the vast majority of the participants who come into this program are able to graduate out of extreme poverty, at which point we see that they are more than ready for more commercial microfinance. The ultra-poor program, being a grant-based program, requires funding. It cannot be commercially viable like microfinance programs typically are.[5]

Abed describes how connecting to the ultra-poor required BRAC to move beyond the microfinance framework. Engaging directly with the ultra-poor allowed BRAC to better understand their daily experience and develop ways to reach them with new programs.

When Vancity Credit Union in British Columbia launched its Fair & Fast Loan program as an alternative to payday loans, its process was similar. Archana Ananthanarayan describes how understanding the experiences of its members allowed Vancity to design a financial product that has the intended impact:

To develop Fair & Fast, we used a user-centric design process. That means we stepped into the shoes of those who use payday lending in order to understand what they need, and we co-created Fair & Fast with them. One learning that surprised us was that many people felt embarrassed at needing to take out a payday loan, and would go to great lengths to keep it a secret. We met people who would go to payday lenders in a different city so that their neighbors wouldn't see them. Some people would go to the payday lender late at night, after their family was asleep. That's when we decided we needed to create an online version of the Fair & Fast Loan that our members can use at home any time of the day.[6]

Integrating a System Perspective

Integrating a system perspective into an impact assessment process offers an additional leverage point for success. One important argument for adding a system perspective is that it helps the business avoid unintended negative side effects or negative impact. For example, reducing CO_2 emissions by raising the price of gasoline in order to reduce the use of cars might disproportionally affect low-income people who lack alternative transportation options. Even a well-intended intervention can have a negative impact.

This is where the concept of thinking in systems is helpful. Systems thinking became popular after a group of MIT researchers produced the 1972 report *Limits to Growth*.[7] To map the impact of economic actions, the report adopted a system perspective on the environmental state of our world and identified limiting factors that affect the future of our planet. The study introduced the concept of leverage points for change, which the authors defined as "places within a complex system (a corporation, an economy, a living body, a city, an ecosystem) where a small shift in one thing can produce big changes in everything."[8]

The report also described how delayed feedback loops affect systems. For example, my actions have impacts that are distant in time or space from when and where they took place. I pollute the air today by driving my old diesel car through the streets of Cambridge. The impact is felt by the bike rider behind me, and my grandkids will suffer from the accumulated air pollution. But I don't see or feel the impact of my decision here and now. To understand how my action affects others and the system as a whole, I must stop, reflect, and analyze my behavior from a larger perspective.

Three forms of complexity Systems thinking has been influential in how we understand nature, society, and organizations, and has allowed the development of tools and methods to understand and cope with the complexity of systems.

We can think of three forms of complexity: (1) dynamic complexity (delayed feedback in time and space), (2) social complexity (diverse stakeholders, interests, mental models), and (3) emerging complexity (disruptive change).[9]

Dynamic complexity describes the delayed feedback loop between cause and effect. The full impact of an action is delayed in time and space; those who cause the change do not experience its effect, or experience it only later. A whole-system analysis captures the different feedback loops that create the dynamics of a system—for example, connecting car pollution with the biker and the asthma of the young child in the neighborhood. This form of analysis can be done at any level of social reality—the individual, team, or organization—and in a neighborhood, an industry, society, or planetwide. *Limits to Growth* introduced systems analysis to the field of environmental issues. Peter Senge in his best-selling book *The Fifth Discipline* describes how to lead organizations with a systems thinking approach,[10] and systems thinking is being used in many different fields, including in the fight against climate change.[11]

Understanding the complexity of systems requires moving beyond the dynamic complexity that describes delayed feed-back loops, the delay between cause and effect. Many banks deal with social complexity, such as when they work with different stakeholders in order to create impact. The work of Harvard professor Chris Argyris helps us understand how to address social complexity with the help of mental models.[12] Mental models describe how we think and what frameworks and concepts underlie our analysis of the world around us. For example, the discriminatory redlining of minority neighborhoods in the United States, which hindered investments in these communities, was based on decision-makers' mental models, beliefs and thinking about marginalized communities and communities of color. Each time we meet with a client, we bring our own framework with us and apply it to our interpretation of the behavior of others or the purpose of what we are doing. Mental models guide us as individuals, but teams, organizations, and societies also operate according to collective mental models, concepts, and frameworks that influence their interpretation of the world. How we think about the economy, refugees, and climate change influences our actions and how we collaborate. To achieve profound innovation and change, we need to become aware of the mental models we use to explain the world around us and, if necessary, to change how we think about the present and the future.

Social complexity calls for different tools from those used to analyze dynamic complexity. Social complexity requires us to develop the skills of self-reflection and the ability to listen and engage in dialogue. Creating effective spaces for stakeholders to do so requires what we call *social technologies*. Social technologies are skills, tools, and processes that improve the quality of social interactions. All of us have experience with social technologies, which we implement when we facilitate meetings or lead conversations, for example.

Having worked with change processes for a large part of our professional lives, we believe that social technologies are essential skills that determine the success of most interventions. In our work with approximately fifty practitioners around the world through the nonprofit Presencing Institute in Cambridge, Massachusetts, we are advancing the development and practice of social technologies that help people reach their potential by addressing and transforming mental models.

The third type of complexity, emerging complexity, has become particularly relevant in recent years because it deals with disruptive change. Emerging complexity arises when the future is radically different from the past. In moments of disruptive change, experience, past learnings, and the tools and capacities that helped us yesterday no longer apply. They might even be counterproductive when it comes to addressing the challenge in front of us. C. Otto Scharmer, a leading thinker in the field of emerging complexity, has introduced the concept of presencing and a framework that he calls Theory U, which employs tools and processes that allow people and organizations to learn in situations of disruptive change. Theory U enables us to "lead from the emerging future" by engaging in this process.[13]

Addressing these three types of complexity is a starting point for creating impact assessment that integrates a systems analysis.

Four Strategies for Creating Impact

A learning infrastructure and a system perspective are important cornerstones of an effective impact assessment process for evaluating the impact of a Just Banking strategy. Banks have choices when it comes to developing an effective strategy that accelerates their impact. A loan officer in one bank we work with asked the following question about the bank's position as a niche player in the Just Banking industry: "If Bank of America decides to switch to 100 percent recycled paper, would they save more CO_2 than our entire renewable energy program?" As niche players, Just Banking organizations have to decide where and how to focus their resources to have the most meaningful impact.

To maximize impact, a Just Banking institution must develop a strategy that meets the needs of its community (the context). As we see it, it has four options, with differing levels of complexity:

Strategy 1: Isolated Social or Green Business Projects and Practices

A large financial player switching to recycled paper is an example of an isolated social or green initiative. The strategy may be implemented by a corporate social responsibility

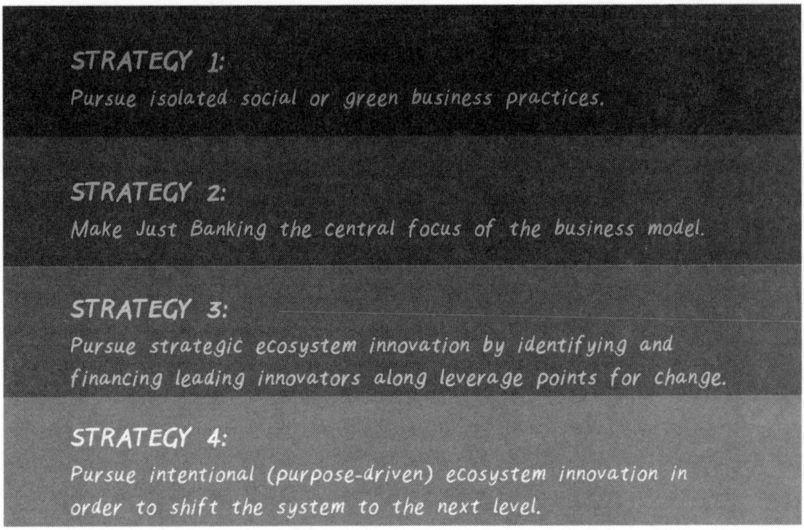

STRATEGY 1:
Pursue isolated social or green business practices.

STRATEGY 2:
Make Just Banking the central focus of the business model.

STRATEGY 3:
Pursue strategic ecosystem innovation by identifying and financing leading innovators along leverage points for change.

STRATEGY 4:
Pursue intentional (purpose-driven) ecosystem innovation in order to shift the system to the next level.

Figure 4.2
Four impact strategies

department, but the bank does not otherwise consider social and environmental impact as decisive criteria in its core operations. The purpose of such an initiative might be to improve branding, motivate and engage employees, respond to stakeholder demands, or take advantage of a business opportunity with an environmentally sustainable or green product. The practice is not core to the overall business. Although it has a positive social or environmental impact, the activity is isolated.

Strategy 2: Just Banking at the Core of the Business Model
When impact is central to the business model, the brand, the relationship with clients, and the profitability of the business

all depend on this strategy. It is not something "nice to have" or an add-on; instead, the activities of this impact strategy are aligned with the purpose of the business through its organizational structure, organizational processes, and leadership. This strategy distinguishes Just Banking players in the market, although no bank is 100 percent socially responsible or green. There is always a gap.

To ensure they do not deviate from their impact objectives, many banks identify minimum criteria and processes that define a boundary the organization is not willing to cross. For example, Triodos Investment Management (TIM) uses the following process when considering an investment:

Step 1: Set minimum criteria. All companies are assessed against minimum criteria. Activities that exclude a company from Triodos investments include gambling, nuclear power generation, weapons manufacture, genetic engineering, and factory farming. Process-related exclusion criteria include violations of labor or human rights and corruption. On its website, Triodos also posts position papers on specific subjects, such as animal testing, human rights, and nuclear power.

Step 2: Identify a business's sustainable activities. Companies that derive at least 50 percent of their revenue from sustainable activities qualify for inclusion in Triodos investments.

Step 3: Further evaluate companies that do not meet the criterion of step 2 (50 percent sustainable activities) but are identified as "best in class"; they may still qualify for

Triodos investment. To evaluate this potential, companies are screened according to more than seventy sector-specific criteria.

The implementation of these three steps establishes the conditions for investment by an organization in which impact is central to the business model.

Strategy 3: Strategic Ecosystem Innovation That Identifies Leverage Points for Change

Just Banking businesses are niche players in the markets they operate in and must determine how to leverage their impact. Some of these organizations employ "strategic ecosystem innovation." This strategy requires identifying and focusing on leverage points in the system. A leverage point can be an innovation that changes an industry, an entrepreneur who enters a new market, or a missing element in a community development process. Answering the following questions can be helpful:

1. Who are the innovators in the market?
2. What elements are missing from the system, such as the value chain, the market, or the neighborhood?
3. Who holds a strategically important role?

GLS Bank in Germany funded one of the first solar-electric boats that transport tourists on the Spree River in Berlin. The decision was made to support this fast-growing sector in Germany's capital by financing the company that introduced a renewable energy solution. GLS's head of sustainable economy, Andre Meyer, described the bank's investment decision in this way: "We knew that this was the first of its kind. So, we wanted to help prove that solar-electric ships are possible. Our objective is for all ships in our state to run emission-free in a few years. ... We are OK if competitors step in and support this clean way of transportation. The market is big enough and has to change quickly."[14]

The impact strategy underlying this decision is to identify a player in the field who might change how the overall sector—in this case, shipping—operates. It is not about competition but about the opposite. The goal is for the rest of the market to catch on. This strategy is an ecosystem innovation.

The ecosystem innovation strategy requires integrating the following steps:

1. Understand the challenge from a system perspective.
2. Identify leverage points for change and find intervention points in the system.
3. Develop a solution from the perspective of those operating in the system—for example, the loan client in a sector you want to change—and then take the quality-of-life improvement as a guiding principle.
4. Develop a solution that is financially sustainable for both bank and client.

Strategy 4: Intentional (Purpose-Driven) Ecosystem Innovation That Shifts the System to the Next Level

Although identifying leverage points in a system increases impact, a purpose-driven strategy requires expanding the role of banking so that the bank becomes an active player in the ecosystem.

XacBank, based in Ulaanbaatar, the capital of Mongolia, has a mission to provide accessible and transparent financial services to the most marginalized citizens of Mongolia. Ulaanbaatar is the coldest capital city in the world, with temperatures routinely dropping below −30° C in the fall, winter, and spring, and also one of the most polluted cities in the world. Nonetheless, more than 800,000 residents in the city of 1.4 million live in *gers*, felt tents typically used by nomadic herders in the countryside. Ger districts are often deeply impoverished and lack connections to water, electricity, and other crucial elements of urban infrastructure. It is common for ger district residents to heat their tents with inefficient coal-burning furnaces. This leads to two major issues: energy costs often account for a large portion of a family's annual income, and burning coal for heat is a major contributor to the high levels of air pollution in the city.

Fuel-efficient stoves and other methods of ger insulation, such as blankets and door coverings, can be exorbitantly expensive for residents of the ger districts. XacBank, recognizing a need for better and more affordable heating methods, built a network of product centers throughout the ger districts of Ulaanbaatar. These centers sell subsidized energy-efficient and clean-burning heaters in partnership with the Millennium Challenge Corporation and the Clean Air Fund of Mongolia. Through these centers, the bank offers microloans for the purchase of the energy-efficient products. These Eco Consumption Loans are designed to be accessible to the low-income population, offering a low interest rate, flexible repayment plans, and low collateral requirements. On the provider side, XacBank also targets loans to small and medium-sized enterprises producing energy-efficient products.

In addition to establishing the product centers and eco-loans, XacBank has worked with the social enterprise Micro-Energy Credits to calculate and monitor the reduction in carbon emissions that is a direct result of the products they have sold. MicroEnergy Credits buys carbon credits from XacBank and sells them on the mainstream carbon market. XacBank then uses the money from this exchange to further finance and develop its eco-banking programs.

This case illustrates the concept of the intentional ecosystem strategy. The starting point is similar to strategy 3, which is to understand the overall system and the leverage points for change. But it does not stop there. XacBank is creating a collaboration among actors in the system that need each other to devise effective solutions, in this case addressing the inefficient heating systems in gers. Just creating a loan product would not be a solution. XacBank had to partner with a network of stakeholders who collaborated to cocreate the solution.

Engaging in an intentional ecosystem innovation requires the following steps:

1. Understanding the challenge from a system perspective.
2. Identifying leverage points for change.
3. Developing a solution from the perspective of the customer (quality-of-life improvement).

4. Identifying the stakeholders needed to create a solution.
5. Convening stakeholders and facilitating a collaborative solution or approach that works for all parties involved.

This impact strategy requires additional skills from a bank, including the capacity to facilitate stakeholder collaboration. Here is another example that dives deeper into the level of engagement that might be needed when employing a purpose-driven ecosystem impact strategy:

Verity Credit Union joined the Othello Square project, an initiative in South Seattle, a highly diverse district with a large number of refugees, many of whom reside there to escape the high cost of housing in central Seattle. The project was started by Verity employees who were involved with nonprofits in the neighborhood. The employees' engagement connected the credit union with the people who lived there. Building on those connections, Verity decided to take the next step and fully participate in the initiative. Adjacent to the Othello light-rail station in Seattle is a piece of land that was claimed by neighbors to be transformed into a multipurpose center for the community. It took more than two years of regular multi-stakeholder meetings, forums, and workshops for the Othello Square project to take off. The goal is to co-locate affordable retail space, an early learning center, a high school, a business incubator, cooperatively owned and mixed-income housing, a health clinic, and a multicultural center. The project aspires to become an economic and cultural anchor, with more than 350 on-site jobs, health care, education, and ownership possibilities for the residents. From the very beginning of the project, Vivian Valencia, director of community relations at Verity

Credit Union, attended weekly community meetings to better understand how the credit union could serve the neighbors' needs. Valencia's ongoing presence further developed the connection between the community and Verity Credit Union. More than a dozen other partners joined the initiative, including the City of Seattle, King County, the Multicultural Community Coalition (comprising eight smaller ethnic organizations), and the Odessa Brown Children's Clinic on behalf of Seattle Children's Hospital. Verity Credit Union became the preferred lender for the affordable housing cooperative and plans to open a new branch inside one of its four buildings.

This example of a purpose-driven ecosystem strategy illustrates the level of collaboration needed to pursue the strategy. Building the level of trust needed to create an effective collaboration requires personal engagement and a reliable and trusted partner.[15]

Measuring Impact

Once an impact strategy is in place, a bank needs to figure out how to measure its impact. As impact finance grows in importance, the number of promising approaches has also grown. There are many inspiring examples of measuring systems, reporting systems, and impact standards, including the Impact Reporting and Investment Standards (IRIS), the International Integrated Reporting (IR) Framework, the Sustainable Accounting Standards Board (SASB), and the Global Reporting Initiative (GRI), to name a few.[16] All these approaches grapple with balancing quantitative and qualitative criteria, conducting evaluation and self-assessment, ranking results, and introducing learning processes.

Understanding Impact at the Organizational Level: GLS Bank, Germany

Many banks develop their own tools and methods to fit their size and their culture, and to align processes with their impact strategy. GLS Bank in Germany is experimenting with developing its own comprehensive impact measurement system, with the goal of guiding the bank toward systemic impact. What distinguishes this example in the field of impact measurement on the organizational level is the goal to connect the measurement tool with the systemic questions, What is our vision of society? What is the image of our future that we want to create? Answering these questions launches a deep dive into the different impact areas that the bank wants to focus on, such as renewable energy, education, and food.

Let's consider the example of renewable energy. First, GLS Bank developed and described its vision for the renewable energy sector. It researched the sector and conducted a dialogue with loan officers responsible for the sector, with clients in the sector, and with the leadership of the bank. The vision is encapsulated by selected key phrases:

- Growing the renewable energy sector in Germany
- Connecting renewable energy to people
- Decentralization of the sector
- Ensuring a diversity of players
- Supporting efficient and innovative technology

With this list as a starting point, the impact measurement tool gets more detailed for each technology: wind, solar, geo-thermal, biogas, and so on. For each technology, the bank defines its system vision and proposes impact indicators to account for the respective contributions to this vision. By assessing the contributions, relevance, and details of each indicator used, all stakeholders are invited to challenge and discuss the most relevant leverage points to achieve the system vision. System change stories are developed to help chan-nel financing activities and societal debate in the direction needed to create the most impact.

The purpose of this work-intensive process is dual: (1) to ensure that the bank has a systemic societal impact and (2) to engage all levels of the organization, from loan officers to clients to internal and external experts. The effort is led by an internal team in the bank that engages with the different stakeholders. Ideally, the result is a continuous learning pro-cess at all levels and a better understanding of whether and how the investments in renewable energy affect the sector as a whole. This impact assessment focus also helps clients learn and advance their own practices by asking themselves the same question that the bank poses: What is needed, from a sys-tem perspective, to shift Germany toward renewable energy?[17]

The example of GLS Bank illustrates how measuring impact and creating a learning infrastructure go hand-in-hand, and how including the system perspective can guide the develop-ment of an impact measurement process.

Certify and Collaborate

In addition to impact measurement at the level of a single organization, measurement methods have been developed to evaluate impact across several organizations. One example is a certification process. B Corps are businesses certified as balancing purpose and profit. Today, more than three thousand businesses in over sixty-four countries worldwide are certified B Corps.[18] The certification process is organized by the global nonprofit organization B Lab. B Lab reviews the social and environmental performance of the business in several steps and adjusts the process to its size and to the sector the business operates in. The process follows these steps:

1. Impact assessment: The applicant for B Corps certification completes a self-assessment questionnaire that covers the areas of governance, employees, community, environment, and customers and sends it to B Lab.

2. Documentation: If the results of the questionnaire are accepted by B Lab, the applicants submit supporting documentation for review.

3. Interview: A member of B Lab conducts an interview with the applying business based on steps 1 and 2.

4. Background check: B Lab conducts a background check to see whether the self-reported information is correct.

Once certified, B Corps are listed in a B Corp directory and are allowed to call themselves B Corp certified.[19] A new B Corp pays an annual fee and signs a declaration that says it "uses business as a force for good."[20] Certified B Corp companies also commit to change their legal documents to include their commitment to all stakeholders. After certification, B Corps receive a customized improvement plan based on the assessment.

The B Corps impact assessment is a comprehensive tool that integrates a learning component by using the data from the certification process to engage the business in a reflection and improvement process. The B Corps approach focuses less on an impact strategy for leveraging the individual business approaches and more on creating a movement toward social and green business practices. The certification allows members to identify themselves in the market and to attract customers that respond to this objective. B Corps have become a successful global movement.

In the financial sector, the scorecard of the Global Alliance for Banking on Values (GABV) is another assessment tool. With more than sixty members around the world, GABV is a network of banks that use finance as a tool for addressing societal challenges. The alliance has developed a scorecard that lets its members self-assess based on principles of "values-based" banking. The criteria include:

- a client-centered approach;
- triple-bottom-line accounting;
- transparency;
- banking in the real economy (no speculative financial products); and
- long-term resiliency.

The GABV Scorecard is designed for regulated banking institutions, and each section of the self-assessment tool has quantitative and qualitative elements. The scorecard allows members to self-assess their impact and improve their own practices by tracking their progress over time. Similar to B Corps, the GABV aims to create a movement that has a systemic impact.

Understanding Impact at a Societal Level

Finally, let us take a look at the best-known measurement of economic development, gross domestic product (GDP). GDP is just one number that measures the value of goods and services produced by a nation. The GDP framework was developed for a US congressional report in 1934. The economist who wrote the report, Simon Kuznets, immediately warned that GDP should not be used as a key indicator of economic success, a warning that went ignored when, in 1944, the Bretton Woods Conference made GDP the standard for measuring, ranking, and comparing the success of economies.

Critics of GDP object to its use on several grounds:

1. GDP measures only quantity, not quality, which means it does not distinguish repairs and rebuilding after a national disaster from innovating a sustainable business solution.
2. GDP ignores unpaid work, such as taking care of family members.
3. GDP assumes that bigger is better, a growth concept that in times of climate crisis is counterproductive.
4. GDP does not capture quality of life.[21]

If the GDP of two economies is the same, and one economy benefits from exploitation and poverty whereas the other reflects a more equal and sustainable society, the GDP would not capture this distinction.

What is the alternative? Since the 1990s, we have seen several attempts to introduce impact measurement systems on a macrolevel that capture different qualitative factors in society. The United Nations Development Program (UNDP) launched the Human Development Index to capture quality of life as measured by a country's life expectancy at birth, its adult literacy rate, and its standard of living. The World Happiness Report, produced by the UN Sustainable Development Solutions Network, offers an annual index ranking countries on factors such as social support, life expectancy, freedom, trust, and generosity, in addition to income. The Organization for Economic Cooperation and Development (OECD) produces the Better Life Index, which compares well-being across countries based on factors the organization deems essential to quality of life, including housing, community, health, and environment.[22] Bhutan's Gross National Happiness Index captures data on psychological well-being, culture, education, and the environment and no longer includes GDP.[23] All UN member states adopted the seventeen Sustainable Development Goals (SDGs) in 2015. The SDGs are "a universal call to action to end poverty, protect the planet and ensure that all people enjoy peace and prosperity by 2030." The widespread use of the SDGs shows the power of indicators to communicate a common vision.[24]

To return to our starting point, the implementation of impact indicators requires a learning infrastructure that introduces the indicators, measures behaviors, and allows for adjustments. Such an infrastructure can be applied to the individual, organizational, regional, and global levels. The indicators used by an organization reflect what it thinks is important to measure. The use of GDP currently reflects how we think about the economy. Changing the indicators will require changing how we think about economic development and societal well-being.

Learning to Understand Impact

Creating impact goes hand-in-hand with understanding impact. Impact measurement systems can oversimplify by creating simple indicators for complex matters. But we need this simplification of indicators to create a common language, and to measure different points in time. Indicators are always (and only) models of the world that simplify a complex reality. It is therefore important to remain aware of the complexity of reality and to be clear about the assumptions that underlie the indicators in use.

It is necessary to connect with the specifics of the impact—for example, by talking with the residents of the neighborhood, the entrepreneurs, and the loan officers about the specifics of a loan and a client. And we need to take a larger perspective, engage in double-loop learning, and look at situations from a system perspective. Effective impact assessment requires moving fluidly among these three poles. What we cannot do is to stay in one corner of the triangle and assume that we understand the impact of our work. Impact measurement is a movement, an activity, that requires analysis, letting go of assumptions, stepping into concrete experiences, and engaging with the context.

5
Just Money: From Ego-System to Ecosystem Finance

The disruptive challenges we face today are unprecedented. Democracies are under attack, inequality and marginalization are destroying our social fabric, climate change is threatening the very survival of our planet, and a pandemic and its social and economic fall-out threatens the health and livelihood of billions. New approaches and solutions are needed. What we are doing now is no longer working. Four in ten Americans would be unable to come up with $400 in cash reserves in the event of an emergency, according to a 2019 report from the Federal Reserve Board, a statistic that became a devastating reality during the COVID-19 pandemic.[1] The world's ten richest billionaires, according to *Forbes* in 2019, own $745 billion in combined wealth, a sum greater than the value of the total goods and services many nations produce annually.[2] More than one million species of plants and animals are at risk of extinction, with as many as 30 to 50 percent of all species possibly heading toward extinction by mid-century.[3] Climate change has evolved into a climate crisis.

Hans Joachim Schellnhuber, an atmospheric physicist, climatologist, and the founding director of the Potsdam

Institute for Climate Impact Research (PIK), was one of the first to identify climate change as a threat to the global community in the 1970s. In a meeting with some of the bankers we work with, he argued that the climate crisis cannot be addressed without support from the financial sector. We believe this is true for a number of the disruptive challenges we face as a society. Banks will define our future, and without changes in the financial sector, it will be impossible to find or fund solutions.

This book has explored innovators in the financial system that are combining profitability with positive societal impact. The Just Banking model operates according to a logic that challenges the profit-maximizing economic paradigm we live in. Even though this new thinking goes against the current, we are seeing the market for impact-aware financial products grow. More and more consumers and organizations, not just banks, seem to be coming around to the idea that social and climate crises are not going to be fixed by governments and nonprofits alone. Where and how we spend and invest our money matters. This mixing of business with societal responsibility has also taken hold outside the financial sector. Businesses are embracing social causes from climate change to inequality.

The Relationship between Business and Society

Confronted with these crises, the role of business in society, and the relationship between business and society, may be on the brink of change. Giving governments and NGOs the sole responsibility for fixing problems that are caused in large part by how we organize our economies is not a solution. Today's challenges also require the power of the private sector as a force for good.

In June 2019, 181 CEOs of major US businesses released a joint statement specifying the purpose of companies as serving not only shareholders but also other stakeholders, including customers, staff, suppliers, and their communities.[4] This announcement marks a notable departure from the status quo. Commenting on this statement, the *Economist* reflected the mainstream argument: business is about competition, not about fixing societal problems. Noting the small percentage of society that owns shares in large businesses, it questioned the right of the CEOs of the largest US firms to decide what societal issues need to be addressed and to whom they should be accountable. What CEOs consider a worthwhile cause might not reflect what society needs but rather what these CEOs need to grow their own business. The *Economist* writers argued that corporations already contribute to society by providing goods and services, as well as jobs.[5] This is a valid point: unlike government, businesses do not have a democratic mandate to decide what causes should be prioritized. That said, the opportunity to leverage the entrepreneurial players to accomplish positive change cannot be missed. It will be a crucial element of any long-term solution. The *Economist* raises an important issue that should not shut the door on businesses shifting their focus away from shareholder wealth maximization but rather should raise new questions, many of which we discuss in this book. At a minimum, businesses should understand their impact and take responsibility for it. Even more, they can help find innovative solutions for societal problems and build a business case around them. This is what Just Banking institutions and impact-aware businesses do.

Innovating from an Ecosystem Perspective

When the first science of climate change emerged in the 1970s, and the subsequent catastrophe of Chernobyl exposed the risk of nuclear energy, the Netherlands-based Triodos Bank and Germany's GLS Bank began to develop financial products that created investment opportunities in renewable energy, an idea that is mainstream today. Southern Bancorp, a community development financial institution, provides innovative financial solutions for local businesses that create jobs in the Mississippi Delta of the United States, and Vancity Credit Union in Vancouver, Canada, builds on user-centered design principles to create a financial product that helps its low-income members break out of the downward spiral of payday lending. Just Banking institutions are prototyping a shift in the banking business model from impact-unaware to impact-aware, and demonstrating how to take a societal challenge as a starting point for building a business model.

More and more businesses are beginning to integrate impact awareness into their operations. The public debate about the role of business and the impact of our economic system is growing. The number of publications, conferences, and presentations on such topics as rethinking capitalism and the new economy are indicators of this trend.[6]

From Ego-System to Ecosystem Awareness

Economic systems evolve over time. We need only consider the shift from preindustrialized economies in Europe to the first Industrial Revolution in the late eighteenth century, and how the economic logic shifted from centralized coordination of the economy dominated by a few heads of state to a decentralized free market system.[7] The result was astonishing. The new freedom created an explosion of market activity and growth. Freed of restrictions devolving from a centralized system and a limited number of players, individuals became entrepreneurs who could make use of opportunities and their own labor. But the shadow side continued. Exploitation of labor and environmental destruction created misery and human suffering. In economic theory, these effects are referred to as the negative externalities of the free market system.

When stakeholder groups begin to form around these negative externalities—for example, around labor issues—a third form of coordination emerges. Stakeholder engagement appears. Labor unions fight for better working conditions. NGOs form to address social and environmental issues and push back against the growing power of business. The European economic model has settled on this regulated market approach, whereas in the United States the debate over the role of government in regulating the economy is an ongoing political battle.

Just Banking institutions, as well as social businesses in other sectors of the economy, introduce a fourth logic, the logic of ecosystem awareness. The urgent need to address and mitigate the negative externalities of a free market system can only partly be handled by a complex stakeholder negotiation process or government intervention. Social businesses and Just Banking institutions have recognized this limitation and aim to create business innovations that address societal challenges that are also financially self-sustaining. When the business objectives of Just Banking institutions introduce a positive societal impact into the equation, they no longer fit the dominant economic paradigm of profit maximization. This fourth logic incorporates an intentional shift from focusing on just the business (ego-system awareness) to focusing on the ecosystem in which the business operates. The ecosystem can be the community the bank serves or the society the bank wants to see move toward carbon neutrality to fight climate change. This also requires new collaborations among NGOs, government, and business. While the first three models describe existing economic models, this fourth model of ecosystem economies, we believe, is emerging, and Just Banking institutions are a part of it.

We have divided the past and future of our economic system into four primary coordination mechanisms. Though these mechanisms are not completely distinct or linear over time, we see that each additional economic logic requires new skills and practices. Table 5.1 summarizes this evolution.

Table 5.1
Evolution of the economic logic toward ecosystem awareness

Stage	Description	Example	Logic	Advantages	Challenges
1.0	Centralized, state-centric	17th-century Europe, state socialism	Hierarchy and control	Stability	Lack of freedom
2.0	State + market (two sectors, decentralized markets)	Industrialization; laissez-faire economics; neoliberalism	Ego-system awareness	Entrepreneurship (markets and competition)	Negative externalities
3.0	State + market + NGOs (three sectors, conflicting)	European social markets	Stakeholder processes	Combines entrepreneurship with restricting negative externalities	Slow negotiation processes, after the fact
4.0	The commons (three sectors, cocreating)	Emerging new economic model: social entrepreneurship, Just Banking	Ecosystem awareness	Entrepreneurial solutions for societal challenges	Complexity; new social skills required

Source: Otto Scharmer and Katrin Kaufer, *Leading from the Emerging Future: From Ego-System to Eco-System Economies* (San Francisco: Berrett-Koehler Publishers, 2013).

Underlying each logic are different societal, organizational, and personal attributes. Centralized economies are coordinated through a hierarchy that is based on power and traditional leadership. Free markets require the skills, capacity, and motivation to act entrepreneurially. Regulated markets require stakeholder engagement and negotiations, as well as dialogue skills. Ecosystem awareness requires an intentional shift away from an ego-system perspective to an ecosystem awareness and builds on people's ability to operate in complex systems.

From Ego-System to Ecosystem Finance

The Just Banks described in this book will not change the financial system. Their model is scalable, but not to a degree that will transform the financial sector as a whole. Their market share is too small and the dominant financial actors are too powerful. But the niche players presented here are challenging the traditional thinking about finance and banking with their business model, and in doing so they are questioning the fundamental role of finance in society. They are not satisfied with the idea that banks fulfill their role in society by, as the *Economist* suggests, providing financial services, creating jobs, and maximizing profits.

The cases in this book provide insight into what the next iteration of financial institutions might look like—businesses that innovate from an ecosystem perspective. In ecosystem finance the well-being of society is one of the core drivers of the innovation process. Just Banking institutions offer learnings about new business practices, but they also identify leverage points for shifting the financial system. The following sections identify some of these leverage points for moving from ego-system to ecosystem finance.

Assess the Success of the Financial Sector from the Perspective of Society

The purpose of the nonfinancial economy is to provide goods and services. The purpose of finance is to facilitate financial transactions for nonfinancial actors. In our current system, the financial sector and its profits are growing disproportionally in comparison with the rest of the economy. A large number of financial products are disconnected from the real economy of goods and services and are speculative in nature. The logic of who should serve whom is turned upside down.

Shifting toward ecosystem finance requires assessing the effectiveness of the financial sector in terms of how well it serves the real economy and the needs of the broader society. Financial institutions that operate with an ecosystem logic do not use profitability as the sole indicator of their success. To assess how and to what degree the financial sector succeeds in fulfilling that role requires new indicators and new regulation, but also a new understanding of the role of finance in society.

Implement a Regulatory Approach That Rewards Positive Impact

If the role of the financial sector is seen through the lens of society as a whole, regulations need to reflect that. Financial products that speculate with food prices or bet on the collapse of currencies are disruptive and destabilize society. Regulatory frameworks that support a shift toward ecosystem finance integrate the impact of financial institutions on society into the regulatory framework. Current regulation often does the opposite. Small and impact-aware financial institutions struggle with regulatory demands that do not take the institutions' societal impact into account. Large financial players use their lobbying power to create a regulatory environment that benefits them.

Impact-aware regulations will also need to incorporate a new way to think about risk management. Although regulators are beginning to ask for environmental risk assessments and corresponding reporting practices, the systemic challenges of understanding impact and risk will require innovations in accounting and reporting standards.

Rethink the Economic Model

The current mainstream economic paradigm is highly influenced by neoliberal economics. This paradigm, which is taught in schools and universities, defines academic careers and influences policy decisions but does not provide solutions to the crises we are facing. Social and environmental crises are labeled negative externalities, and the tasks of addressing them are typically assigned to governments, NGOs, and foundations. As with any powerful system, our current economic paradigm reinforces itself with mental models about profit, growth, and individualism that are deeply ingrained in our politics and culture. Much of the work of moving from ego-system to ecosystem finance involves dismantling these concepts and developing new skills, new ways of operating, and even a new economic vocabulary. We cannot solve the existing problems without articulating a new economic model.

There is a thriving and ongoing discourse in search of a new economic model; some rubrics here include "circular economy" and "regenerative economy." All these approaches recognize the need to move away from profit maximization and a never-ending growth model, and many integrate new ideas derived from biological processes and observations of the natural world. Just Banking institutions learn from these models, but they also play an important role in prototyping and testing these theories in practice.

This requires both adopting an ecosystem perspective and intentionally shifting toward impact awareness. The moment businesses take responsibility for their impact, they begin to operate with the logic of ecosystem awareness, stepping into the perspective of the ecosystem in which the business operates. For a small bank, this could be the local community; for a green bank, it could be the energy sector.

Innovate Business Operations from an Ecosystem Perspective

Just Banking institutions need to anchor this perspective and its impact objectives in their organization through their governance system, their operational structure, and their leadership. But the daily operation of a business from an ecosystem perspective is substantively different from, and often more complex than, the daily operation of a traditional business. In response to this complexity, Just Banking institutions have developed new organizational practices for running a business from an ecosystem perspective. How do you compensate and measure performance when the business objective is not maximizing profit? How do you measure and evaluate your impact? How do you communicate with your clients and depositors about your impact? These are questions that must be answered if a Just Banking institution is to anchor its mission and make impact the core of its business model. Ecosystem finance—and all impact-aware businesses—must reinvent their operations to reflect this expanded mission

Learn How to Understand Impact

Measuring and communicating impact is critical to the success of a Just Banking institution. Such institutions need to develop impact measurement tools that fit both their business model and the ecosystem in which they operate. An impact measurement approach driven by a system perspective goes beyond capturing how much the bank's investments contribute to reducing the CO_2 footprint, for example. A system perspective leads banks to ask how they can proactively contribute to solving the climate crisis and seeking leverage points for change through a deeper analysis of the ecosystem. Any impact measurement tools used should attempt to capture this system impact.

The success of any impact measurement system also depends on what happens with the indicators once they are identified. Who should look at them? How should they be discussed and interpreted? What action should come next? Impact measurement needs to be combined with an effective learning infrastructure that creates structured space for learning and reflection. This can happen in a meeting, at a retreat, or in a dialogue space. The quality of the learning space depends on the social and communication skills of the participants—for example, the quality of listening they bring to the space.

Upgrade the Monetary System So That It Serves Societal Well-Being

Will our future monetary system be designed by Facebook? The national bank of Sweden and the national bank of China are exploring cryptocurrencies to be used in parallel with the existing currency system.[8] A citizen initiative in Switzerland proposed putting a sovereign money system on the ballot, aiming to give the Swiss National Bank the sole authority to create money.[9] Although the initiative was rejected, it launched a debate about why retail banks have the authority to issue money when they issue a loan.[10]

The questions of what money is and who controls it are central to the discussion about upgrading our financial system. Banks and financial institutions are important players in the economy because they deal with all forms of money. Economies depend on a functional financial system that facilitates monetary transactions effectively.

The existing monetary system has evolved over centuries, defined both by economic and political decisions and by technological and cultural changes. Given the dysfunctionality of the current financial system, we have the option to wait for it to collapse, or we can be proactive and begin the process of rethinking money. Historical events such as the Bretton Woods Conference after the end of World War II prove that the process of designing the monetary system and its governing institutions is negotiable. A similar process today would address only the current challenges if (unlike at Bretton Woods in 1947) the voices of the marginalized and the voices of the future were represented at the table. A redesign of the existing monetary system needs to determine how the financial system can best serve the real economy, who should sit at the table when reforms are discussed, and what technologies are needed. One can imagine a type of constitutional assembly tasked with rewriting the rules.

Develop Ecosystem Leadership Capacities

Our experience running a leadership development program for high-potential leaders in Just Banking institutions revealed that leading with an ecosystem perspective requires distinct skills. Leadership is not the same as management, which focuses on developing operational methods to achieve goals. One definition of "to lead" is "to go forth"; another is "to cross a threshold."[11] According to that definition, leadership should entail stepping into the unknown and the new. Leaders of Just Banking institutions need to understand and communicate why they are doing this new work, why they want to take responsibility for stepping into this new territory. Ecosystem leadership implies that leaders are aware of their personal intentions, which are anchored in their personal values and their life journey. Ecosystem-based businesses should expect a leader to step into a system perspective. Systems are complex and interdependent. Ecosystem leadership is based on the ability to see and sense these systems, and to act from the perspective of the whole.

Advance Financial Education

Many of the banks we work with offer financial education to their customers and communities. The impact of financial education can be life-changing. It is important for individuals, families, and communities to understand how their financial decisions will affect their futures. But financial education related to ecosystem finance goes beyond individual finances and includes a public debate on the future of the financial system.

The complexity of financial products today—the speed with which they are disseminated, their global reach, and the language used to discuss them—can hinder this public debate on the purpose and limitations of the financial sector. But there are ways to dissolve these barriers. When the US Consumer Financial Protection Bureau proposed that every mortgage contract in the United States summarize all essential decisions required by the contract on its first page, it was met with an outcry that the inherent complexity of a mortgage contract would make this impossible. But it worked.

Financial education builds the capacity of everyone to manage her or his finances, but also to open up the black box that is called a "the financial sector" and look for accountability and transparency. Ecosystem finance raises the lid on this black box and shines a light inside.

Use Digitization for Impact

Emerging digital technologies raise hopes for decentralizing and possibly democratizing finance. Although the biggest investors in financial digitization are large banks and financial institutions, a wide range of newcomers around the globe are joining in. Fintech companies have plucked specific financial products and services from the banking sector and created businesses around providing them quickly and at low cost, without the institutional bulk or regulatory burden of a bank. Digitization has changed banking and will continue to change it in the coming years.

In an ecosystem-based financial sector, digitization provides a host of new and exciting opportunities. Cryptocurrencies designed for specific communities,[12] crowdfunding and lending circles, financial services designed to reach marginalized communities, and platforms that leverage social innovators (e.g., platform.coop), among other innovations, have the potential to create positive, wide-reaching impact. Though there is much talk of digital disruption in the banking sector as new players emerge, the underlying logic that defines the current financial system also in large part defines digital financial innovations. The learnings in this book about the relationship between finance and impact apply. New technologies might increase the efficiency and accessibility of finance, but using digitization as a force for positive change requires anchoring the digital solutions in an intention to do so and developing structures of systemwide accountability. The experience of Just Banking institutions reveals that technology does not create solutions; the impact is created by the underlying intention that drives its use. This intention defines the outcome as well as the impact on society. And the intention needs to be anchored in the governance system, the operations, and the leadership of the organization.

What Kind of Banking Does the Future Need?

In setting out to write this book, we wanted to explore whether Just Banking practices and innovations could inform the next iteration of our financial system, and if so, how. We hoped to contribute to a discussion about what kind of banking our future needs. Finance defines our future with every investment decision we make. What is funded or not writes the story of what the future will look like.

The challenges societies face today raise many questions about the future role of finance and about the relationship between finance and society. The current system is unstable and dysfunctional, and systems theory teaches us that unstable systems do not last. Governments and NGOs on their own are not in a position to solve the problems created by our financial and economic systems.

The next iteration of our economic system needs to measure its success against the well-being of all. We believe that this will require upgrading to an ecosystem economy, one centered on the impact of the system on society and one that prioritizes the well-being of all. This means that the innovation power of business must be directed toward solving society's problems. But its success will depend on the collaboration among all sectors—business, government, and nonprofit organizations.

We are far from possessing the skills and building the institutions required for an economy that is based on ecosystem thinking. But the examples in this book provide some insight into the kinds of innovation that will be necessary. Rethinking finance will be one of the most important cornerstones in the transition to an ecosystem economy. The types of financial institution described here cannot create stability on their own, but they demonstrate how the financial system can address pressing issues. Their innovations show what a financial system that serves the whole could look like. To quote the founder of Germany's GLS Bank, "We can only overcome our fear of a future that we are anxious about with an image of a future that we want."[13] This vision of the future we want to create is already palpable.

Acknowledgments

Our thanks go first to Dayna Cunningham, executive director of MIT CoLab (Community Innovators Lab), who encouraged and enabled us to design the online MIT edX course Just Money: Banking as if Society Mattered. Dayna, your powerful vision for a just and equitable economy and your work on economic democracy and overcoming marginalization were the inspiration for this book.

Our next thanks go to Otto Scharmer, MIT Sloan School senior lecturer and cofounder of the Presencing Institute. Otto, your leadership and your inspirational thinking on Ecosystem concepts and frameworks but also your bold initiatives on how to create democratic infrastructures for transforming society and self are ground-breaking. Thank you for believing in a future where the economy serves everyone and thank you for focusing your work on processes and practices that enable societal transformation.

We thank Phil Thompson for cocreating the MIT edX course. You pushed our thinking, and your work sets the benchmark for translating ideas into reality.

We also want to thank our colleagues—or, better, our "family" at MIT CoLab and the Presencing Institute. The work all of you do is why we wrote this book. You also allowed us to step out of our daily routine and write. In the MIT Cambridge office, thanks are owed to Antonio Moya-Latorre, Jillian Kronberg, Juan Constain Ramos, Shey Rivera, and Taina S. McField, and in New York and Colombia, thanks go to Aly Bryson, Katherin Gill, Katherine Mella, Maggie Tishman, Milady Garces, Natalia Mosquera, Nick Shatan, and Yorman Nuñez.

Thanks to the Presencing Institute team that stepped up for Katrin while we were writing: Angela Baldini, Becky Buell, Florentina Bajraktari, Janice Spadafore, and Kelvy Bird. Additional thanks to Kelvy Bird for designing the figures in this book. And thanks to the amazing Presencing Institute practitioners around the world who work to improve the lives of so many every day: Adam Yukelson, Aggie Kalungu-Banda, Antoinette K, Klatzky, Arawana Hayashi, Carmen Chacra, Eva Pomeroy, Jayce Pei Yu Lee, Julie Arts, Katie Stubley, Lily Xu, Marian Goodman, Mercedes Bidart, Olaf Baldini, Rachel Hentsch, Sarina Bouwhuis, and Simon Fransen.

Thanks to the banks around the world that are creating financial innovations. Special thanks to the banks of the Global Alliance for Banking on Values (GABV.org). Thanks to the bankers who devote their lives to showing that a different form of banking is possible and who became generous thinking and interview partners for this book: Sir Fazle Hasan Abed, Juan Pablo Mezza, Martin Rohner, Mary Houghton, Peter Blom, Shameran Abed, Tamara Vrooman, and Thomas Jorberg.

Special thanks to Martin Kalungu-Banda and Sonia Reinhard for cofacilitating the GABV Leadership Academy and supporting our vision of learning spaces for values-based bankers. We so love our work together, and we learned so much from both of you. We are looking forward to our next projects together! Thanks to Els Verhagen, who was not only one of our lead thinking partners in trying to understand what it requires to translate Just Banking into daily operation but who supported our research in so many countless ways and inspired many of the concepts presented here.

Thanks to our student team: Alice Maggio, Lafayette Cruise, and Zoë Ackerman. You are amazing and your commitment to change society makes us trust into the future. Thanks to all those whom we interviewed for the MIT edX online program and the case studies that were part of this research. And finally, we thank Jason Spicer for his support and contributions to the early stages of the work.

Thanks to all participants in the GABV Leadership Academy. You are our inspiration and why we do this work! Thanks to the Human Development Track of the GABV, who innovate on a daily basis mission-based organizational practices. Special thanks to Janina Zajic, Robert Farmer and Florence Maweijje for their ongoing support and for the outstanding work you are doing. Also our many thanks to everyone in the GABV Secretariat.

We also want to thank Janet Mowery, our amazing editor, who was always there during a compressed timeline. And thanks to Emily Taber of the MIT Press for inviting us to write this book.

From Katrin ...

I thank Gabriel Lutz, Martin Butzlaff, Kerstin and Christian von Plessen, and Britta Lenders for your ongoing support, and for a push at the right moment. Thanks to Hannah and Johan for supporting the writing with uplifting comments.

Last but not least, I thank Otto for commenting on several drafts of the manuscript, challenging our ideas, encouraging new thinking, and supporting the manuscript to its completion. Not sure there would be a book without you.

—Katrin

Cambridge, Massachusetts, January 2020

From Lillian ...

I thank my parents, Laurie and Vin, and my sister Elena. Your support means the world to me.

—Lillian

Oakland, California, January 2020

Notes

Introduction

1. B Corporation certification is issued by the global nonprofit organization B Lab after evaluation of social and environmental performance (see https://en.wikipedia.org/wiki/B_Corporation_(cer tification); see also https://bcorporation.net/certification).

Chapter 1

1. The website for Triodos Bank can be found at https://www .triodos.com/know-where-your-money-goes.

2. The formal name is Vancouver City Savings Credit Union, but we use Vancity Credit Union as a shorthand throughout the book.

3. For information about the Vancity Fair & Fast Loan, see the website https://www.vancity.com/Loans/TypesOfLoans/FairAndFastLoan.

4. Pew Research Center, "Remittances from Abroad Are Major Economic Assets for some Developing Countries" (Washington, DC: Pew Research Center, January 29, 2018), https://www .pewresearch.org/fact-tank/2018/01/29/remittances-from-abroad -are-major-economic-assets-for-some-developing-countries.

5. BRAC, "BRAC Ranked Number One NGO Two Years in a Row," January 9, 2017, accessed August 8, 2019, http://www.brac.net

/component/k2/item/1010-brac-ranked-number-one-ngo-two-years
-in-a-row.

6. Peter Quartey, Ebo Turkson, Joshua Y. Abor, and Abdul M. Iddrisu, "Financing the Growth of SMEs in Africa: What Are the Constraints to SME Financing within ECOWAS?," *Review of Development Finance* 7, no. 1 (2017): 18–28; Laura Vasilescu, "Accessing Finance for Innovative EU SMEs: Key Drivers and Challenges," *Economic Review: Journal of Economics and Business* 12, no. 2 (2014): 35–47; World Bank Group, "What's Happening in the Missing Middle? Lessons from Financing SMEs," n.d., https://www.worldbank.org/en/topic /financialsector/publication/whats-happening-in-the-missing-middle -lessons-from-financing-smes.

7. Otto Scharmer and Katrin Kaufer, *Leading from the Emerging Future: From Ego-System to Eco-System Economies* (San Francisco: Berrett-Koehler Publishers, 2013).

8. Tamara Vrooman, interview, in the course materials for "Just Money: Banking as if Society Mattered," MITX, 11.405x, https:// courses.edx.org/courses/course-v1:MITx+11.405x+2T2019/course.

9. Ian MacPherson, *Hands around the Globe: A History of the International Credit Union Movement and the Role and Development of World Council of Credit Unions, Inc.* (Victoria, BC: Horsdal & Schubart Publishers & WOCCU, 1999).

10. For more on the Glass-Steagall Act, see the website https://www .federalreservehistory.org/essays/glass_steagall_act.

11. European Commission, "Sustainable Finance," https://ec.europa .eu/info/publications/180308-action-plan-sustainable-growth_en.

12. Federal Deposit Insurance Corporation, "2017 FDIC National Survey of Unbanked and Underbanked Households," https:// www.fdic.gov/householdsurvey.

13. World Bank Group, "Financial Inclusion on the Rise, but Gaps Remain, Global Findex Database Shows," press release, April 19,

2018, https://www.worldbank.org/en/news/press-release/2018/04
/19/financial-inclusion-on-the-rise-but-gaps-remain-global-findex
-database-shows.

14. Richard Taub, *Community Capitalism* (Boston: Harvard Business
School Press, 1988); Richard Taub, *Doing Development in Arkansas:
Using Credit to Create Opportunity for and with Entrepreneurs outside the
Mainstream* (Fayetteville: University of Arkansas Press, 2004).

15. One early pioneer in the fight against redlining was Shore Bank
in Chicago, which was founded to address the impact of redlining
in that city and later served as a model for others, such as Southern
Bancorp in Arkansas and Mississippi. It also had a global impact,
leading to the founding of BRAC Bank, among other examples.

16. Thomas Jorberg, interview, in the course materials for "Just
Money: Banking as if Society Mattered," MITX, 11.405x, https://
courses.edx.org/courses/course-v1:MITx+11.405x+2T2019/course.

17. Jorberg, interview, in the course materials for "Just Money."

18. Peter Blom, interview, in Triodos Bank, *Integrated Annual
Report 2018*, https://www.annual-report-triodos.com/en/2018.

19. Triodos Bank, "Our Vision on Impact," https://www.triodos.com
/vision-on-impact.

20. Amy Domini, interview, in the course materials for "Just
Money: Banking as if Society Mattered," MITX, 11.405x, https://
courses.edx.org/courses/course-v1:MITx+11.405x+2T2019/course.

21. Triodos Investment Management, "How We Invest Defines
the World We Want to Live In," https://www.triodos-im.com.

22. Quoted in Katrin Kaufer, "Banking as if Society Mattered: The
Case of Triodos Bank," MIT Working Paper (Cambridge, MA: MIT
CoLab, 2011).

23. Personal conversation with the authors, May 2019.

24. Personal conversation with the authors, August 2019.

25. Quoted in Kaufer, "Banking as if Society Mattered," 35.

26. See also William McDonough and Michael Braungart, *Cradle to Cradle* (New York: North Point Press, 2002); Janine M. Benyus, *Biomimicry: Innovation Inspired by Nature* (New York: HarperCollins, 1998).

27. Peter Blom, interview, in the course materials for "Just Money: Banking as if Society Mattered," MITX, 11.405x, https://courses.edx.org/courses/course-v1:MITx+11.405x+2T2019/course.

28. Living wage is defined as the minimum income necessary to cover a worker's basic needs.

29. Personal conversation with the authors, September 2018.

30. Simon Johnson and James Kwak, *13 Bankers: The Wall Street Takeover and the Next Financial Meltdown* (New York: Random House, 2011).

31. Simon Johnson, interview, in the course materials for "Just Money: Banking as if Society Mattered," MITX, 11.405x, https://courses.edx.org/courses/course-v1:MITx+11.405x+2T2019/course.

Chapter 2

1. Thorsten Schmitz, "Bayerische Sparkasse mischt bei Mieterverdrängung in Berlin mit," *Süddeutsche Zeitung,* July 12, 2019.

2. Action research was first described by MIT's Kurt Lewin in 1944. It links research, transformative change, and action together with a process of critical reflection. Kurt Lewin, *Group Decision and Social Change* (New York: Holt, Rinehart and Winston, 1958); Peter Reason and Hilary Bradbury, *The Sage Handbook of Action Research: Participative Inquiry and Practice* (Thousand Oaks, CA: Sage, 2008).

3. Stefan Schaltegger and Roger Burritt, "Business Cases and Corporate Engagement with Sustainability: Differentiating Ethical Motivations," *Journal of Business Ethics* 147, no. 2 (2018): 241–259; Michael L. Barnett, "Stakeholder Influence Capacity and

the Variability of Financial Returns to Corporate Social Responsibility," *Academy of Management Review* 32, no. 3 (2007); David Vogel, *The Market for Virtue: The Potential and Limits of Corporate Social Responsibility* (Washington, DC: Brookings Institution Press, 2005).

4. Quoted in Katrin Kaufer, "Banking as if Society Mattered: The Case of Triodos Bank," MIT Working Paper (Cambridge, MA: MIT CoLab, 2011), https://www.colab.mit.edu/resources.

5. Suzanne Young and Vijaya Thyil, "Corporate Social Responsibility and Corporate Governance: Role of Context in International Settings," *Journal of Business Ethics* 122, no. 1 (June 2014): 1–24.

6. Deepa Seetharaman, "Ford Chairman Nearly Doubles Stake in Supervoting Shares—Filing," *Reuters Market News,* June 26, 2013, https://www.reuters.com/article/autos-ford-family/ford-chair man-nearly-doubles-stake-in-supervoting-shares-filing-idUSL2N0F 219I20130626.

7. Council of Institutional Investors, "Dual-Class IPO Snapshot: 2017–2018 Statistics," April 3, 2018, https://www.cii.org/files /Board%20Accountability/2018Q1%20IPO%20Stats%20for%20 Website.pdf.

8. Vijay Govindarajan et al., "Should Dual-Class Shares Be Banned?," *Harvard Business Review*, December 3, 2018.

9. Josh Baron, "Is Your Company's Strategy Aligned with Your Ownership Model?," *Harvard Business Review,* January 25, 2019.

10. Quoted in Kaufer, "Banking as if Society Mattered," 57.

11. See Triodos Bank, "Sustainable Banking according to Triodos Bank," https://www.triodos.com/governance.

12. Quoted in Kaufer, "Banking as if Society Mattered," 61.

13. BRAC Bank has 50 percent institutional shareholders, including BRAC (33.51 percent), International Finance Corporation (9.5

percent), and Shore Cap International (6.99 percent). Since early 2007, the remaining halves of its shares have been distributed to the general public and mutual funds through its IPO on the Dhaka and Chittagong Stock Exchanges.

14. Brian Argrett, interview, in the course materials for "Just Money: Banking as if Society Mattered," MITX, 11.405x, https://courses.edx.org/courses/course-v1:MITx+11.405x+2T2019/course.

15. "Eigentum verpflichtet. Sein Gebrauch soll zugleich dem Wohle der Allgemeinheit dienen," 14 Abs. 2 Grundgesetz (German Constitution, Article 14, Paragraph 2).

16. Manfred Brocker, *Eigentum und Arbeit* (Darmstadt: WBG Academic Publisher, 1992).

17. Cesare Vitale, interview, in the course materials for "Just Money: Banking as if Society Mattered," MITX, 11.405x, https://courses.edx.org/courses/course-v1:MITx+11.405x+2T2019/course.

18. Vitale, interview, in the course materials for "Just Money."

19. Edgar Schein, *Organizational Culture and Leadership* (San Francisco: Jossey-Bass, 2010), 23–33.

20. Schein, *Organizational Culture and Leadership*.

21. Colin Cuthbert, interview, in the course materials for "Just Money: Banking as if Society Mattered," MITX, 11.405x, https://courses.edx.org/courses/course-v1:MITx+11.405x+2T2019/course.

22. Els Verhagen, Triodos Bank, Netherlands, personal conversation with the authors, March 2018.

23. Verhagen, personal conversation, March 2018.

24. Quoted in Katrin Kaufer, "Values-Based Banking Reinvents Human Resource Management: A Handbook," paper presented at the GABV Annual Meeting, March 2018, 18.

25. This practice would be illegal in the United States, although in this case it is set up as a support system for coworkers who have greater financial needs because of their specific social context.

26. The GABV Leadership Academy was designed by heads of impact banks in 2015 and has run annually since then with twenty-five to thirty high-potential leaders from impact banks around the world. Katrin Kaufer is one of the cofacilitators.

27. C. Otto Scharmer, *The Essentials of Theory U: Core Principles and Applications* (Oakland, CA: Berrett-Koehler Publishers, 2018).

28. Scharmer, *The Essentials of Theory U*.

29. Authors' conversation with Dayna Cunningham, June 2016, during module II of the GABV Leadership Academy.

Chapter 3

1. Gerald Epstein, ed., *Financialization and the World Economy* (Northampton, MA: Edward Elgar, 2005); Richard B. Freeman "It's Financialization!," *International Labour Review* 149, no. 2 (2010): 163–183.

2. Christopher Witko, "How Wall Street Became a Big Chunk of the U.S. Economy—and When the Democrats Signed On," *Washington Post*, March 29, 2016; Deloitte Insights, "Changing the Lens: GDP from the Industry Viewpoint," *Economics Spotlight*, July 2019, https://www2.deloitte.com/us/en/insights/economy/spotlight/economics-insights-analysis-07-2019.html#.

3. Greta R. Krippner, *Capitalizing on Crisis: The Political Origins of the Rise of Finance* (Cambridge, MA: Harvard University Press, 2012); Simon Johnson and James Kwak, *13 Bankers: The Wall Street Takeover and the Next Financial Meltdown* (New York: Random House, 2011).

4. Stephen G. Cecchetti, and Enisse Kharroub, "Why Does Financial Sector Growth Crowd Out Real Economy Growth?," BIS Working Paper 490 (Brussels: Bank for International Settlements, Monetary and Economic Department, February 2015), https://www.bis.org/publ/work490.pdf; Leila Davis, "Financialization, Shareholder Value and the Cash Holdings of U.S. Corporations," *Review of Political Economy* 30, no. 1 (2018): 1–27.

5. Milton Friedman, "The Social Responsibility of Business Is to Increase Its Profits," *New York Times Magazine*, September 13, 1970, 32.

6. Note that regulation is determined by national and international legislation.

7. National Credit Union Administration, "Historical Timeline," https://www.ncua.gov/about-ncua/historical-timeline.

8. National Credit Union Administration, "Quarterly Credit Union Data Summary, 2019, Q1," https://www.ncua.gov/files/publications/analysis/quarterly-data-summary-2019-Q1.pdf.

9. Susan Hoffmann, *Politics and Banking: Ideas, Public Policy and the Creation of Financial Institutions,* (Baltimore, MD: Johns Hopkins University Press: 2001).

10. Samantha Cristobal, "4 Ways Credit Union Market Share Is Growing," *Industry Insights* (blog), CreditUnion.com, August 28, 2018, https://www.creditunions.com/blogs/industry-insights/4-ways-credit-union-market-share-is-growing/#ixzz5xZUXtfbPhttps://www.creditunions.com/blogs/industry-insights/4-ways-credit-union-market-share-is-growing.

11. William R. Emmons and Frank A. Schmid, "Credit Unions Make Friends—But Not with Bankers," Federal Reserve Bank of St. Louis, October 1, 2003, https://www.stlouisfed.org/publications/regional-economist/october-2003/credit-unions-make-friendsbut-not-with-bankers; Gina Hall, "Bankers Say Credit Union Rule Reaches Too Far," *Business Journals: Banking and Financial Services,*

December 8, 2016, https://www.bizjournals.com/bizjournals/news
/2016/12/08/bankers-say-credit-union-rule-reaches-too-far.html.

12. Mehrsa Baradaran, *The Color of Money: Black Banks and the
Racial Wealth Gap* (Cambridge, MA: Harvard University Press,
2017), 76, 83.

13. Clifford N. Rosenthal, *Democratizing Finance: Origins of the Community Development Financial Institutions Movement* (Victoria, BC:
Friesen Press, 2018).

14. David Caplovitz, *The Poor Pay More. Consumer Practices of Low-
Income Families* (New York: Free Press of Glencoe, 1963).

15. Rosenthal, *Democratizing Finance,* 47–60; Richard Taub, *Community Capitalism* (Boston: Harvard Business School Press, 1988);
Katrin Käufer, *Geldinstitute im Spannungsfeld zwischen monetärem
und gesellschaftlichem Erfolg* (Wiesbaden: Gabler Verlag, 1996).

16. Connie E. Evans, "Eliminating the CDFI Fund Would Harm
Black Entrepreneurship," *Forbes*, June 1, 2017.

17. City First Bank is a CDFI that operates as a private financial
institution to serve a local community.

18. Brian Argrett, interview, in the course materials for "Just
Money: Banking as if Society Mattered," MITX, 11.405x, https://
courses.edx.org/courses/course-v1:MITx+11.405x+2T2019/course.

19. Chase Woodruff and David Sirota, "Is Goldman Sachs' New
Fund Really Just Greenwashing Stocks?," *Guardian,* September 28,
2018, 76, https://www.theguardian.com/business/2018/sep/28/is
-goldman-sachs-new-fund-really-just-greenwashing-stocks

20. Paul Hawken, "The Truth about Ethical Investing," *The Tyee*,
May 19, 2005, https://thetyee.ca/Citizentoolkit/2005/05/19/Truth
EthicalInvesting; Jasper Jolly, "Just How Ethical Is Ethical Invest-
ment?," *Guardian*, February 22, 2019; Paul Brest and Kelly Born,
"Unpacking the Impact in Impact Investing," *Stanford Social*

Innovation Review, August 14, 2013, https://ssir.org/articles/entry
/unpacking_the_impact_in_impact_investing#.

21. John Elkington, *Cannibals with Forks: The Triple Bottom Line of
21st-Century Business* (Oxford: Capstone, 1999).

22. John Elkington, "25 Years Ago I Coined the Phrase 'Triple
Bottom Line': Here's Why It's Time to Rethink It," *Harvard Business
Review,* June 25, 2018.

23. Ivo Knoepfel, ed., *Who Cares Wins: Connecting Financial
Markets to a Changing World* (Swiss Federal Department of Foreign Affairs and United Nations, 2005), https://www.unepfi.org
/fileadmin/events/2004/stocks/who_cares_wins_global_com
pact_2004.pdf.

24. UN PRI, "What Are the Principles for Responsible Investment?," https://www.unpri.org/pri/an-introduction-to-responsible
-investment/what-are-the-principles-for-responsible-investment.

25. Rockefeller Philanthropy Advisors, "Impact Investing: An
Introduction," 2017, https://www.rockpa.org/wp-content/uploads
/2017/10/RPA_PRM_Impact_Investing_Intro_WEB.pdf.

26. Rockefeller Philanthropy Advisors, "Impact Investing."

27. Charles Piller, Edmund Sanders, and Robyn Dixon, "Dark Cloud
over Good Works of Gates Foundation," *Los Angeles Times*, January
7, 2007; Ameet Sachdev, "Money and Mission: When Investments
Conflict with Philanthropy," *Chicago Tribune*, September 19, 2014.

28. Matt Bannick, Paula Goldman, Michael Kubzansky, and Yasemin Saltuk, "Across the Returns Continuum," *Stanford Social
Innovation Review,* Winter 2017.

29. George Ingram and Robert A. Mosbacher Jr. "Development
Finance: Filling Today's Funding Gap," brief for the 15th Annual
Brookings Blum Roundtable, "Challenges to and Opportunities
for U.S. Foreign Assistance and Global Leadership," July 31, 2018,

https://www.brookings.edu/research/development-finance-filling
-todays-funding-gap.

30. Claire Provost, "The Rise and Fall of Microfinance," *Guardian*, November 21, 2012; Aneel Karnani, "Microfinance Misses Its Mark," *Stanford Social Innovation Review*, Summer 2007.

31. Shameran Abed, interview, in the course materials for "Just Money: Banking as if Society Mattered," MITX, 11.405x, https://courses.edx.org/courses/course-v1:MITx+11.405x+2T2019/course.

32. Soutik Biswas, "India's Microfinance Suicide Epidemic," *BBC News*, December 16, 2010, https://www.bbc.com/news/world-south-asia-11997571.

33. Personal conversation with Lillian Steponaitis, El Salvador, March 2015.

34. The respective websites are, for Worldcoo, https://www.worldcoo.com; for M-Pesa, https://www.moneygram.com/us/en/send-money-to-kenya?gclid=EAIaIQobChMImL3Oyuju5gIVjIbACh1slwsAEAAYASAAEgILgPD_BwE&gclsrc=aw.ds; for Omisego, https://omisego.co; and for Quipu Market, https://www.quipumarket.com.

35. World Bank Group, "Migration and Remittances: Recent Development and Outlook," *Migration and Development Brief* 29 (April 2018): 11; World Bank Group, "Accelerated Remittances Growth to Low- and Middle-Income Countries in 2018," press release, December 8, 2018, https://www.worldbank.org/en/news/press-release/2018/12/08/accelerated-remittances-growth-to-low-and-middle-income-countries-in-2018.

36. Shamima Yesmin, Tonmoy Ananda Paul, and Md. Mohshin Uddin, "bKash: Revolutionizing Mobile Financial Services in Bangladesh?," in *Business and Management Practices in South Asia*, ed. Arijid Sikdar and Vijay Pereira (Singapore: Palgrave Macmillan, 2019), 125–148.

Chapter 4

1. Florian Berg, Julian F. Kölbel, and Roberto Rigobon, "Aggregate Confusion: The Divergence of ESG Ratings," MIT Sloan Research Paper 5822–19 (Cambridge, MA: MIT, Sloan School of Management, August 2019), https://ssrn.com/abstract=3438533.

2. Donella H. Meadows, *Thinking in Systems: A Primer* (White River Junction, VT: Chelsea Green Publishing, 2008), 11.

3. Chris Argyris, "Single-Loop and Double-Loop Models in Research on Decision Making," *Administrative Science Quarterly* 21, no. 3 (1976): 363–375.

4. Antonia Ward, Ellie Runcie, and Lesley Morris, "Embedding Innovation: Design Thinking for Small Enterprises," *Journal of Business Strategy* 30, no. 2/3 (2009): 78–84.

5. Shameran Abed, interview, in the course materials for "Just Money: Banking as if Society Mattered," MITX, 11.405x, https://courses.edx.org/courses/course-v1:MITx+11.405x+2T2019/course.

6. Archana Ananthanarayan, presentation to the GABV Leadership Academy, Berlin, October 2017.

7. Donella Meadows, Dennis L. Meadows, Jørgen Randers, and William W. Behrens, *The Limits to Growth; A Report for the Club of Rome's Project on the Predicament of Mankind*, 2nd ed. (New York: Universe Books, 1972).

8. Donella Meadows, "Leverage Points: Places to Intervene in a System" (Hartland, VT: Sustainability Institute, 1999).

9. C. Otto Scharmer, *Theory U. Leading from the Future as It Emerges* (San Francisco: Berrett-Koehler Publishers, 2009), 58.

10. Peter Senge, *The Fifth Discipline: The Art and Practice of the Learning Organization* (New York: Doubleday, 1990).

11. John D. Sterman, "System Dynamics Modeling: Tools for Learning in a Complex World," *California Management Review* 43, no. 4 (Summer 2001).

12. Chris Argyris and Donald A. Schon, *Organizational Learning: A Theory of Action Perspective* (Boston: Addison-Wesley, 1978).

13. C. Otto Scharmer, *The Essentials of Theory U: Core Principles and Applications* (San Francisco: Berrett-Koehler, 2018).

14. Personal conversation with Andre Meyer, August 28, 2018.

15. Several personal conversations with Antonio Moya-Latorre and Tina Narron in July and August 2019. We thank Antonio Moya-Latorre for writing this case.

16. The respective websites are, for IRIS, https://iris.thegiin.org; for the International IR Framework, https://integratedreporting .org/resource/international-ir-framework; for the SASB, https:// www.sasb.org; and for the GRI, https://www.globalreporting.org /Pages/default.aspx.

17. Thanks to Jan Köpper for providing detailed information on GLS Bank's impact measurement approach in a conversation with Katrin Kaufer on August 16, 2019.

18. See the B Corps website at https://bcorporation.net.

19. The directory is available at https://bcorporation.net/directory.

20. See the B Corps web page at https://bcorporation.net/about -b-corps.

21. Joseph E. Stiglitz, Jean-Paul Fitoussi, and Martine Durand, *Beyond GDP: Measuring What Counts for Economic and Social Performance* (Paris: OECD Publishing, 2018); C. Otto Scharmer, "Our Obsession with Economic Growth Ignores Everything That Makes Life Worthwhile," *Huffington Post,* Opinion, June 4, 2018, https://www .huffpost.com/entry/opinion-scharmer-gdp-economic-growth_n_5a c6160de4b056a8f598db31.

22. OECD, Better Life Index, http://www.oecdbetterlifeindex.org/#/11111111111.

23. Centre for Bhutan Studies & GNH website can be accessed at http://www.grossnationalhappiness.com.

24. UNDP, "Sustainable Development Goals," https://www.undp.org/content/undp/en/home/sustainable-development-goals.html.

Chapter 5

1. Board of Governors of the Federal Reserve System, *Report on the Economic Well-Being of U.S. Households*, May 23, 2019, https://www.federalreserve.gov/newsevents/pressreleases/other20190523b.htm.

2. Kerry A. Dolan and Luisa Kroll, "Forbes Billionaires 2018: Meet the Richest People on the Planet," *Forbes*, March 6, 2018.

3. Intergovernmental Science-Policy Platform on Biodiversity and Ecosystem Services (IPBES), "Report of the Plenary of the Intergovernmental Science-Policy Platform on Biodiversity and Ecosystem Services on the Work of Its Seventh Session," May 29, 2019, https://www.ipbes.net.

4. Business Roundtable, "Statement on the Purpose of a Corporation," https://opportunity.businessroundtable.org/ourcommitment.

5. "What Are Companies For? Competition, Not Corporatism, Is the Answer to Capitalism's Problems," *Economist*, August 22, 2019, https://www.economist.com/leaders/2019/08/22/what-companies-are-for?frsc=dg%7Ce.

6. Examples are the annual Conscious Capitalism Conference, the Coalition for Inclusive Capitalism, and the New Economy Forum. Books on these issues include Raj Sisodia, Timothy Henry, and Thomas Eckschmidt, *Conscious Capitalism Field Guide: Tools for Transforming Your Organization* (Boston: Harvard Business Review Press, 2018); Paul Collier, *The Future of Capitalism: Facing the*

New Anxieties (New York: HarperCollins, 2018); and Joseph E. Stiglitz, *People, Power, and Profits. Progressive Capitalism for an Age of Discontent* (New York: W. W. Norton, 2019).

7. Meir Kohn, "Economic Development and the Evolution of Government in Pre-Industrial Europe" *SSRN,* December 8, 2005, https://papers.ssrn.com/sol3/papers.cfm?abstract_id=866986.

8. Riksbank website, https://www.riksbank.se/en-gb/payments--cash /e-krona, and https://www.pymnts.com/cryptocurrency/2019/china -central-bank-readying-crypto-launch.

9. Although voters rejected the initiative, it reflects rising concern over whether the monetary system serves its purpose. Similarly, after the financial crisis of2008–2009, the prime minister of Iceland commissioned KPMG to conduct a study of alternative monetary systems. KPMG, *Money Issuance: Alternative Monetary Systems*, a report commissioned by the Icelandic Prime Minister's Office, September 2016, https://assets.kpmg/content/dam/kpmg/is /pdf/2016/09/KPMG-MoneyIssuance-2016.pdf.

10. Michael McLeay, Amar Radia, and Ryland Thomas, "Money in the Modern Economy: An Introduction," *Bank of England Quarterly Bulletin* 2014 Q1, 14.

11. C. Otto Scharmer, *The Essentials of Theory U: Core Principles and Applications* (San Francisco: Berrett-Koehler Publishers, 2018), 29.

12. Shannon Fraley, "This Argentinian City Planner Is Revolutionizing Local Economies for 1.3 Billion People," *Forbes*, September 4, 2019.

13. Wilhelm Barkoff, "Die Angst vor der Zukunft, die wir fürchten, können wir nur überwinden durch Bilder einer Zukunft, die wir wollen," GLS Bank, Jörg Weber, "Um die soziale und ökologische Wirkung ging es der GLS Bank schon immer. Jetzt steht ein Quantensprung an." Der Blog. Wissen, wo Dein Geld wirkt, August 2019, https://blog.gls.de/bankspiegel/bs-2019-1-gute-wirkung.

Bibliography

Argyris, Chris. "Single-Loop and Double-Loop Models in Research on Decision Making." *Administrative Science Quarterly* 21, no. 3 (1976): 363–375.

Argyris, Chris, and Donald A. Schon. *Organizational Learning: A Theory of Action Perspective*. Boston: Addison-Wesley, 1978.

Bannick, Matt, Paula Goldman, Michael Kubzansky, and Yasemin Saltuk. "Across the Returns Continuum." *Stanford Innovation Review*, Winter 2017.

Baradaran, Mehrsa. *The Color of Money: Black Banks and the Racial Wealth Gap*. Cambridge, MA: Harvard University Press, 2017.

Barnett, Michael L. "Stakeholder Influence Capacity and the Variability of Financial Returns to Corporate Social Responsibility." *Academy of Management Review* 32, no. 3 (2007).

Baron, Josh. "Is Your Company's Strategy Aligned with Your Ownership Model?" *Harvard Business Review*, January 25, 2019.

Benyus, Janine M. *Biomimicry: Innovation Inspired by Nature*. New York: HarperCollins, 1998.

Brest, Paul, and Kelly Born. "Unpacking the Impact in Impact Investing." *Stanford Social Innovation Review*, August 14, 2013.

Brocker, Manfred. *Eigentum und Arbeit*. Darmstadt: WBG Academic Publisher, 1992.

Caplovitz, David. *The Poor Pay More: Consumer Practices of Low-Income Families*. New York: Free Press of Glencoe, 1963.

Collier, Paul. *The Future of Capitalism: Facing the New Anxieties*. New York: HarperCollins, 2018.

Davis, Leila. "Financialization, Shareholder Value and the Cash Holdings of U.S. Corporations." *Review of Political Economy* 30, no. 1 (2018): 1–27.

DeVaro, Jed, Nan Mawell, and Hodaka Marika. "Training and Intrinsic Motivation in Nonprofit and For-Profit Organizations." *Journal of Economic Behavior & Organization* 139 (2017): 196–213.

Dolan, Kerry A., and Luisa Kroll. "Forbes Billionaires 2018: Meet the Richest People on the Planet." *Forbes*, March 6, 2018.

Elkington, John. *Cannibals with Forks: The Triple Bottom Line of 21st Century Business*. Oxford: Capstone, 1999.

Elkington, John. "25 Years Ago I Coined the Phrase 'Triple Bottom Line.' Here's Why It's Time to Rethink It." *Harvard Business Review,* June 25, 2018.

Epstein, Gerald, ed. *Financialization and the World Economy*. Northampton, MA: Edward Elgar, 2005.

Evans, Connie E. "Eliminating the CDFI Fund Would Harm Black Entrepreneurship." *Forbes*, June 1, 2017.

Fraley, Shannon. "This Argentinian City Planner Is Revolutionizing Local Economies for 1.3 Billion People." *Forbes*, September 4, 2019.

Freeman, Richard B. "It's Financialization!" *International Labour Review* 149, no. 2 (2010): 163–183.

Friedman, Milton. "The Social Responsibility of Business Is to Increase Its Profits." *New York Times Magazine*, September 13, 1970.

Govindarajan, Vijay, Shivaram Rajgopal, Anup Srivastava, and Luminita Enache. "Should Dual-Class Shares Be Banned?" *Harvard Business Review*, December 3, 2018.

Hoffmann, Susan. *Politics and Banking: Ideas, Public Policy and the Creation of Financial Institutions.* Baltimore, MD: Johns Hopkins University Press, 2001.

Ingram, George, and Robert A. Mosbacher Jr. "Development Finance: Filling Today's Funding Gap." Brief for the 15th Annual Brookings Blum Roundtable, "Challenges to and Opportunities for U.S. Foreign Assistance and Global Leadership," July 31, 2018.

Johnson, Simon, and James Kwak. *13 Bankers: The Wall Street Takeover and the Next Financial Meltdown.* New York: Random House, 2011.

Jolly, Jasper. "Just How Ethical Is Ethical Investment?" *Guardian,* February 22, 2019.

Karnani, Aneel. "Microfinance Misses Its Mark." *Stanford Social Innovation Review,* Summer 2007.

Kaufer, Katrin. "Banking as if Society Mattered: The Case of Triodos Bank." MIT Working Paper. Cambridge, MA: MIT CoLab, 2011.

Kaufer, Katrin. "Values-Based Banking Reinvents Human Resource Management: A Handbook." Paper presented at the GABV Annual Meeting, March 2018.

Käufer, Katrin. *Geldinstitute im Spannungsfeld zwischen monetärem und gesellschaftlichem Erfolg.* Wiesbaden: Gabler Verlag, 1996.

Krippner, Greta R. *Capitalizing on Crisis: The Political Origins of the Rise of Finance.* Cambridge, MA: Harvard University Press, 2012.

Lewin, Kurt. *Group Decision and Social Change.* New York: Holt, Rinehart and Winston, 1958.

MacPherson, Ian. *Hands around the Globe: A History of the International Credit Union Movement and the Role and Development of World Council of Credit Unions, Inc.* Victoria, BC: Horsdal & Schubart Publishers & WOCCU, 1999.

McDonough, William, and Michael Braungart. *Cradle to Cradle.* New York: North Point Press, 2002.

McLeay, Michael, Amar Radia, and Ryland Thomas, "Money Creation in the Modern Economy: An Introduction." *Bank of England Quarterly Bulletin* Q1, March 2014, 14

Meadows, Donella. "Leverage Points: Places to Intervene in a System." Sustainability Institute, Hartland, VT: Sustainability Institute, 1999.

Meadows, Donella H. *Thinking in Systems: A Primer*. White River Junction, VT: Chelsea Green Publishing, 2008.

Meadows, Donella, Dennis L. Meadows, Jørgen Randers, and William W. Behrens. *The Limits to Growth: A Report for the Club of Rome's Project on the Predicament of Mankind*, 2nd ed. New York: Universe Books, 1972.

Piller, Charles, Edmund Sanders, and Robyn Dixon. "Dark Cloud over Good Works of Gates Foundation." *Los Angeles Times,* January 7, 2007.

Provost, Claire. "The Rise and Fall of Microfinance." *Guardian,* November 21, 2012.

Quartey, Peter, Ebo Turkson, Joshua Y. Abor, and Abdul Malik Iddrisu. "Financing the Growth of SMEs in Africa: What Are the Constraints to SME Financing within ECOWAS?" *Review of Development Finance 7*, no. 1 (2017): 18–28.

Reason, Peter, and Hilary Bradbury. *The Sage Handbook of Action Research. Participative Inquiry and Practice*. Thousand Oaks, CA: Sage, 2008.

Rosenthal, Clifford N. *Democratizing Finance: Origins of the Community Development Financial Institutions Movement*. Victoria, BC: Friesen Press, 2018.

Sachdev, Ameet. "Money and Mission: When Investments Conflict with Philanthropy." *Chicago Tribune*, September 19, 2014.

Schaltegger, Stefan, and Roger Burritt. "Business Cases and Corporate Engagement with Sustainability: Differentiating Ethical Motivations." *Journal of Business Ethics* 147, no. 2 (2018): 241–259.

Scharmer, C. Otto. *The Essentials of Theory U: Core Principles and Applications*. Oakland, CA: Berrett-Koehler Publishers, 2018.

Scharmer, C. Otto. *Theory U. Leading from the Future as It Emerges*. Oakland, CA: Berrett-Koehler Publishers, 2009.

Scharmer, Otto, and Katrin Kaufer. *Leading from the Emerging Future: From Ego-System to Eco-System Economies*. San Francisco: Berrett-Koehler Publishers, 2013.

Schein, Edgar. *Organizational Culture and Leadership*. San Francisco: Jossey-Bass, 2010.

Schmitz, Thorsten. "Bayerische Sparkasse mischt bei Mieterverdrängung in Berlin mit." *Süddeutsche Zeitung*, July 12, 2019.

Senge, Peter. *The Fifth Discipline: The Art and Practice of the Learning Organization*. New York: Doubleday, 1990.

Sisodia, Raj, Timothy Henry, and Thomas Eckschmidt. *Conscious Capitalism Field Guide: Tools for Transforming Your Organization*. Boston: Harvard Business Review Press, 2018.

Sterman, John D. "System Dynamics Modeling: Tools for Learning in a Complex World." *California Management Review* 43, no. 4 (Summer 2001).

Stiglitz, Joseph E. *People, Power, and Profits. Progressive Capitalism for an Age of Discontent*. New York: W. W. Norton, 2019.

Stiglitz, Joseph E., Jean-Paul Fitoussi, and Martine Durand. *Beyond GDP: Measuring What Counts for Economic and Social Performance*. Paris: OECD Publishing, 2018.

Taub, Richard. *Community Capitalism*. Boston: Harvard Business School Press, 1988.

Taub, Richard. *Doing Development in Arkansas: Using Credit to Create Opportunity for and with Entrepreneurs outside the Mainstream*. Fayetteville, AR: University of Arkansas Press, 2004.

Thompson, Philip. *Double Trouble: Black Mayors, Black Communities, and the Call for a Deep Democracy*. Oxford: Oxford University Press, 2005.

Thompson, Phillip. "Place Matters, and So Does Race." *Urban Affairs Review* 53, no. 1 (2016): 210–218.

Vasilescu, Laura. "Accessing Finance for Innovative EU SMEs: Key Drivers and Challenges." *Economic Review: Journal of Economics & Business* 12, no. 2 (2014): 35–47.

Vogel, David. *The Market for Virtue: The Potential and Limits of Corporate Social Responsibility*. Washington, DC: Brookings Institution Press, 2005.

Walk, Marlene, and Troy Kennedy. "Making Nonprofits More Effective: Performance Management and Performance Appraisals." In *The Nonprofit Human Resource Management Handbook: From Theory to Practice*, ed. Jessica K. A. Word and Jessica E. Sowa. New York: Routledge, 2017.

Ward, Antonia, Ellie Runcie, and Lesley Morris. "Embedding Innovation: Design Thinking for Small Enterprises." *Journal of Business Strategy* 30, no. 2/3 (2009): 78–84.

Witko, Christopher. "How Wall Street Became a Big Chunk of the U.S. Economy—and When the Democrats Signed On." *Washington Post*, March 29, 2016.

Woodruff, Chase, and David Sirota. "Is Goldman Sachs' New Fund Really Just Greenwashing Stocks?" *Guardian*, September 28, 2018.

World Bank Group. "Migration and Remittances. Recent Development and Outlook." *Migration and Development Brief* 29 (April 2018): 11.

Yesmin, Shamima, Tonmoy Ananda Paul, and Md. Mohshin Uddin. "bKash: Revolutionizing Mobile Financial Services in Bangladesh?"

In *Business and Management Practices in South Asia*, ed. by Sikdar A. Pereira, 125–148. Singapore: Palgrave Macmillan, 2019.

Young, Suzanne, and Vijaya Thyil. "Corporate Social Responsibility and Corporate Governance: Role of Context in International Settings." *Journal of Business Ethics* 122, no. 1 (June 2014): 1–24.

Further Reading

Ant Financial. "Alipay Gallery: Ant Forest Tree-Planting Spring 2019." Ant Financial, April 30, 2019. https://medium.com/@AntFinancial/alipay-gallery-ant-forest-tree-planting-spring-2019-dc4e0578cc7c.

Baker, H. Kent, and John R. Nofsingern, eds. *Socially Responsible Finance and Investing. Financial Institutions, Corporations, Investors, and Activists*. Hoboken, NJ: John Wiley, 2012.

Beslik, Sasja. "Could Sustainable Investing Be the Best way to Tackle Climate Change?" World Economic Forum, March 1, 2018. https://www.weforum.org/agenda/2018/03/could-this-be-the-best-way-to-tackle-climate-change-sustainable-investment.

Beslik, Sasja. "Did Project Drawdown Miss a Crucial Climate Solution?" *GreenBiz Webcasts*, March 23, 2018. https://www.greenbiz.com/article/did-project-drawdown-miss-crucial-climate-solution.

Bhandari, Avishek, and David Javakhadze. "Corporate Social Responsibility and Capital Allocation Efficiency." *Journal of Corporate Finance* 43 (April 2017): 354–377.

Connaker, Adam, and Saadia Madsbjerg. "The State of Socially Responsible Investing." *Harvard Business Review*, January 17, 2019.

Desilver, Drew. "Remittances from Abroad Are Major Economic Assets for Some Developing Countries." Washington, DC: Pew

Research Center, January 29, 2018. https://www.pewresearch
.org/fact-tank/2018/01/29/remittances-from-abroad-are-major
-economic-assets-for-some-developing-countries.

Eccles, Robert G., Ioannis Ioannou, and Georg Serafeim, "The Impact of Corporate Sustainability on Organizational Processes and Performance." *Management Science* 60 (2014): 2835–2857.

Ferguson, Niall. *The Ascent of Money: The Financial History of the World*. London: Penguin Books, 2008.

Garrett-Scott, Shennette. *Banking on Freedom. Black Women in U.S. Finance before the New Deal*. New York: Columbia University Press, 2019.

Hakimi, Sherry. "Why Purpose-Driven Companies Are Often More Successful." *Fast Company,* July 21, 2015. https://www
.fastcompany.com/3048197/why-purpose-driven-companies-are
-often-more-successful.

Henderson, Rebecca. *Reimagining Capitalism in a World on Fire*. New York: PublicAffairs, 2020.

Khan, Mozaffar, George Serafeim, and Aaron Yoon. "Corporate Sustainability: First Evidence on Materiality." *Accounting Review* 91, no. 6 (November 2016): 1697–1724.

Nicholls, Alex, Rob Paton, and Jed Emerson, eds. *Social Finance*. New York: Oxford University Press, 2016.

Piketty, Thomas. *Capital in the Twenty-First Century*. Cambridge, MA: Belknap Press of Harvard University Press, 2014.

Smillie, Ian. *Freedom from Want*. Sterling, VA: Kumarian Press, 2009.

US SIF and US Sustainable Investment Foundation. "Report on US Sustainable, Responsible and Impact Investing Trends 2018." https://www.ussif.org/files/Trends/Trends%202018%20execu
tive%20summary%20FINAL.pdf.

US Forum for Sustainable Investment Foundation. "Sustainable Investing Assets Reach $12 Trillion." Press release, October 31, 2018. https://www.ussif.org/files/US%20SIF%20Trends%20Report%20 2018%20Release.pdf.

Weber, Olaf, and Blair Feltmate. *Sustainable Banking and Finance: Managing the Social and Environmental Impact of Financial Institutions*. Toronto: University of Toronto Press, 2016.

Index